Vikings in England

An Enthralling Guide to the Great Heathen Army and the Viking Raids, Wars, and Settlement in Britain

© Copyright 2024 - All rights reserved.

The content contained within this book may not be reproduced, duplicated, or transmitted without direct written permission from the author or the publisher.

Under no circumstances will any blame or legal responsibility be held against the publisher, or author, for any damages, reparation, or monetary loss due to the information contained within this book, either directly or indirectly.

Legal Notice:

This book is copyright protected. It is only for personal use. You cannot amend, distribute, sell, use, quote, or paraphrase any part, or the content within this book, without the consent of the author or publisher.

Disclaimer Notice:

Please note the information contained within this document is for educational and entertainment purposes only. All effort has been executed to present accurate, up-to-date, reliable, and complete information. No warranties of any kind are declared or implied. Readers acknowledge that the author is not engaging in the rendering of legal, financial, medical, or professional advice. The content within this book has been derived from various sources. Please consult a licensed professional before attempting any techniques outlined in this book.

By reading this document, the reader agrees that under no circumstances is the author responsible for any losses, direct or indirect, that are incurred as a result of the use of the information contained within this document, including, but not limited to, errors, omissions, or inaccuracies.

Free limited time bonus

Stop for a moment. We have a free bonus set up for you. The problem is this: we forget 90% of everything that we read after 7 days. Crazy fact, right? Here's the solution: we've created a printable, 1-page pdf summary for this book that you're reading now. All you have to do to get your free pdf summary is to go to the following website:

https://livetolearn.lpages.co/enthrallinghistory/

Once you do, it will be intuitive. Enjoy, and thank you!

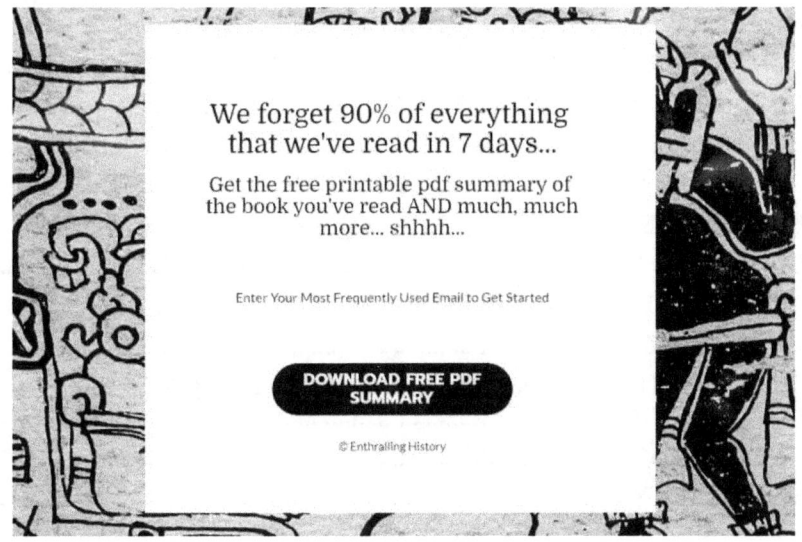

Table of Contents

INTRODUCTION 1
CHAPTER ONE: THE FIRST VIKING RAIDS (780-850 CE) 3
CHAPTER TWO: RAGNAR LOTHBROK 16
CHAPTER THREE: THE GREAT HEATHEN ARMY 24
CHAPTER FOUR: ALFRED THE GREAT 35
CHAPTER FIVE: THE DANELAW 43
CHAPTER SIX: EDWARD AND ÆTHELSTAN 53
CHAPTER SEVEN: SWEYN FORKBEARD AND CNUT THE GREAT 67
CHAPTER EIGHT: STAMFORD BRIDGE AND HASTINGS 79
CHAPTER NINE: LIFE OF A VIKING IN ENGLAND 89
CONCLUSION 97
HERE'S ANOTHER BOOK BY ENTHRALLING HISTORY THAT YOU MIGHT LIKE 100
FREE LIMITED TIME BONUS..101
BIBLIOGRAPHY 102

Introduction

Once upon a time, many years ago, a group of bearded men decided to go on an adventure that would allow them to visit a distant land and make a profit. They hopped in a boat with a dragon's head and rode out to the open sea, where they unfurled their sails and set off. A week or so later, they sighted land, hopped off their boat, and proceeded to burn, pillage, and rape their way through the community before they got back on their ship. This is not a Grimm Brothers' fairy tale or some myth from ancient sagas. This episode happened repeatedly in England during the Middle Ages. Those bearded men were not Santa or his helpers either; they were Vikings, and they were people that you did not want to play around with.

The Vikings were notorious pirates in the Middle Ages. People were in fear of them and what they were capable of doing. However, we must remember that much of what we once knew about the Vikings came from clergymen who were victims of Viking assaults. They portrayed the Vikings as senseless brutes. Fortunately, considerable research has diminished the monastic disinformation campaign, and we have a clearer picture of who these men were.

England was a principal target for Viking raids, and the Vikings created a great deal of disruption. However, these terrors of the high seas were markedly different from earlier sea raiders. Unlike the Sea People of the Bronze Age, Vikings made significant contributions to England's culture and language. They were also prominent in the commerce of the time period. The picture we now have of them is very different from what the monks once portrayed in their manuscripts.

In this book, we will be exploring the Vikings and their impact on England. We will be looking at who the Vikings were, why they chose England as a place to attack, their impact on the politics of the time, and what contributions they made to English society. Make no mistake; we admit that the Vikings caused a great deal of damage. However, an objective observer must admit that the sea rovers left a legacy behind that enriched England and other areas where they settled.

The Vikings' story is a fascinating tale comprised of facts and legends in equal measure. Understanding their deeds and their legacies enables us to gain a deeper appreciation of the forces that shaped medieval society. We can also gain greater insights into how the English language developed and how some of the legal and commercial customs we take for granted were initiated. The Vikings created more than they ever destroyed.

Chapter One: The First Viking Raids (780–850 CE)

The Vikings are often portrayed as ruthless warriors who terrorized Europe in the early medieval period. Although the Vikings are known for their many conquests, the Viking raids on England stand out for their ferocity and impact on English history. From 780 to 850 CE, Vikings made numerous incursions into England, raiding monasteries, towns, and cities, eventually establishing their own kingdoms. These events played a crucial role in shaping the history of England and the Viking Age.

The Doom Carrier: The Viking Drakkar

The Vikings relied on surprise and speed to be successful. A raid was a rather simple affair; they determined a target, landed close to it, attacked, pillaged, and then left as fast as possible. Typically, the Vikings came and went before any relief force was able to assist the region being attacked.

The greatest asset that the Vikings possessed was the ships on which they sailed. These were capable of outrunning any vessel the British kings had. What the Vikings designed were the most innovative boats of the Middle Ages.

And it was not just one particular craft. The Vikings had different types of longships. Let's look at a few of them:

- Karvi

The karvi was a smaller longship and could be used as a trade and transportation vessel. The karvi was equipped with thirteen rowing benches. Because it could handle shallow waters, it was ideal for transport and cargo. The best example we have of a karvi longship is the Gokstad ship. Discovered in 1880, it measures over twenty-three meters (a little over seventy-eight feet) in length.

- Snekkja

The English translation of snekkja is "snake," and that was how quick it was in the water. It had a minimum of twenty rowing benches and could carry a rowing crew of forty men. The standard snekkja was approximately seventeen meters (about fifty-five feet) long. It was a boat that was perfect for Atlantic expeditions. The snekkja was able to handle stormy weather and rough seas, which was essential for any journey across the North Atlantic.

- Skeid

The skeid was one of the larger Viking vessels. It was a warship that had thirty or more rowing benches. A skeid was excavated in the late 20th century that measured 37 meters (over 121 feet) long.

- Drakkar

The drakkar is the classic dragon ship of the Vikings. It stands out because of its elaborate carvings and the dragon head that is positioned on the bow. These ships were constructed to have thirty or more rowing benches.[1]

Design

The Viking longship was narrow and light, with a shallow draft designed specifically for speed. That shallow draft permitted navigation in water that could be as shallow as one meter. The design of the boat permitted beach landings, and its light weight allowed it to be carried over portages. An important feature of the longship was its double-ended design. The symmetrical bow and stern allowed the ship to reverse direction quickly without having to turn around. This was useful in raids, but this design had safety in mind. The North Sea was full of ice floes and other types of ice that were hazardous to shipping. A Viking boat

---

[1] Discover Middle Ages. (2023, August 31). *Viking Ships*. Retrieved from Discovermiddleages.co.uk: https://www.discovermiddleages.co.uk/medieval-life/viking-ships.

could back out and navigate without any trouble, unlike other sea vessels.

The longships were made from oak timbers, with the bow and stern rising three to four meters high. The hull was approximately five meters wide. Amazingly, there were no standard blueprints for the longships. Instead, the shipbuilders would rely on previously built vessels. The ship was built from the keel up.

Keels and sterns were made first and then the strakes, which were lines of planks joined endwise from stern to stern. A common design was the clinker, which had each hull plank overlapping the next. When the planks reached the desired height, the shipbuilders added an interior frame and crossbeams. The keel was narrow and deep, which provided strength beneath the water line. Waterproofing was done with animal hair, wool, hemp, or moss that was drenched in pine tar.

The sails were made from rough wool cloth and held in place by a mast that was up to sixteen meters tall. A side rudder was used to steer the boat. The average speed of these ships was from five to ten knots; the maximum speed in fair weather was approximately fifteen knots. Not only could a Viking ship sail safely across treacherous waters to get to its destination, but it could also outrun any vessel seeking to attack it.

Construction of a skeid longship.
Marit Synnøve Vea, CC BY-SA 3.0 <https://creativecommons.org/licenses/by-sa/3.0>, via Wikimedia Commons;
https://commons.wikimedia.org/wiki/File:DRAKEN_HARALD_H%C3%85RFAGRE._9._BORDGANG_SNART_P%C3%85_PLASS.jpg

Navigation

Vikings were able to cross vast stretches of ocean that did not have identifiable landmarks. Navigators would rely on experience, but there were some rudimentary navigation instruments that we believe the Vikings used to make their voyages successful.

Historians believe that Vikings used a sun compass. This instrument shows the correct direction and basically is a vertical pointer on a horizontal surface. The shadow of the pointer moves throughout the day. It forms a curve that is different at different latitudes and at different times of the year.

Problems arose on cloudy days. Vikings had to have some way of navigating when the weather was bad. Viking sagas speak of sunstones. These were minerals that could polarize light and determine the direction of the sun under cloud cover. To date, there has been no archaeological evidence of sunstones.[2]

Viking Weapons

Ragnar Lodbrok (more about him later) would have gone into battle equipped with some of the best weapons possible. What the local farmers or militia had was no match for what the Vikings carried as personal equipment. If one implement did not kill you, a Viking could easily use another to dispatch you.

A burial excavation at Woodstown, Ireland, gives us an understanding of Viking weaponry in the mid-9th century. The grave was of a warrior buried with all of his weapons. His personal arsenal included a sword, shield, spear, ax, and knife. These were the essential tools of war.

A man's sword took pride of place. These were treasured, and a man would pass down his sword to his son unless the sword was buried with a man. The blades were made of iron, meaning whoever had a sword was rich enough to afford the expense of creating it, although Vikings would also loot swords from the body of a dead enemy. The sword would be approximately ninety centimeters long and include a ten-centimeter tang, which was covered by the handle.

The process for creating a Viking sword was nearly as elaborate as a Japanese samurai sword. Strips of wrought iron were welded together,

---

[2] Thomsen, M. H. (2023, August 10). *Instrument navigation in the Viking Age.* Retrieved from Vikingeskibs Muskeet: https://www.vikingeskibsmuseet.dk/en/professions/education/knowledge-of-sailing/instrument-navigation-in-the-viking-age.

twisted, and hammered out to shape the blade and given a hardened steel edge. Blades were tapered toward the point, and a blood groove was forged along the length. The swords were double-edged and were used for slashing. The Vikings even named their swords. Norse sagas mention blades called War-Snake, Viper, Dragon Slayer, and Widow-Maker.

Spears were standard. Because spears were easier to make, they are often found in large numbers at Viking burial sites. Spears were used for thrusting and throwing. The spears that were thrown would have small heads, while a broader, leaf-shaped head would be used as a stabbing weapon.

Axes had long handles. The ax heads had blades eight to sixteen centimeters long. They were elaborately decorated and permitted the warriors to have a long reach in battle. An experienced ax handler was a deadly force on the field.

Viking shields were nearly one meter wide with a central hole for an iron boss. An iron grip was attached to the boss on the inner face. These protective circles were decorated in bright colors and were the primary defense for Vikings.

Bow and arrows were used, but few fragments have been found so far. An arrow would be around fifteen centimeters long, and bows could be used for hunting as well as fighting.

Helmets were not the stuff of Wagnerian opera. No, Viking helmets did not have horns on the side. The Gjermundbu helmet, which was found in Norway, was an iron cap with four spokes and had a rim with a heavy eye and nose guard attached. Vikings did use chainmail, but this protective covering was very expensive to make. The nobility and elite warriors probably had chainmail, and some Vikings probably robbed corpses of their chainmail on the battlefield.

The Viking raids in England were characterized by their speed and the use of surprise tactics. In many cases, the Vikings would strike quickly, taking advantage of the element of surprise to catch their enemies off-guard. They would use the longship as a means of transport, attacking their targets along the coast and then sailing away before any resistance could be mounted. Their tactics were brutal, often involving the massacre of entire populations.

Perhaps the most famous Viking raid was when the Vikings attacked the monastery of Lindisfarne in 793 CE.

Lindisfarne

Monasteries in 7th-century England were places where men would gather in a communal society to worship and praise the Lord. They were places of extreme piety, and people would go there to renounce the world and seek the road to salvation, which was a major thought in most people's minds at the time. The nobility of the era sought to burnish their reputation by endowing monks with property, which the pious men used to build monasteries. King Oswald of Northumbria did this in 635 CE when he endowed an Irish monk named Aidan with a small island called Lindisfarne.

This speck of ground in the North Sea was six miles north of the Northumbrian capital of Bamburgh. The solitude that the monks looked for on Lindisfarne was enhanced by the causeway, which the tide covered twice each day, assuring a sense of isolation but also a connection to the mainland.

Lindisfarne's reputation was enhanced in the 670s when a monk named Cuthbert became part of the community. Cuthbert was a saint of early England and became the bishop of Lindisfarne. He became well connected to the Northumbrian court and was generally liked by everybody. His death caused Lindisfarne to be a pilgrimage site, as a cult grew up around his holiness. That brought dramatic changes to the secluded community.

After Lindisfarne became a major pilgrimage site in northeastern England, pilgrims went there to seek the aid and blessings of St. Cuthbert. They left behind more than just good wishes; many pilgrims made donations and left rich gifts to the monastery and its monks. Lindisfarne became important and rich. It had no fortifications, though, and the monks still led simple lives in the midst of great wealth. It had a reputation not only for sanctity but also for its treasures. Frankly, Lindisfarne was a pigeon waiting to be plucked. And that is what happened in 793.[3]

Viking Assault

This was not the first Viking raid on England. There was a smaller incursion a few years before in Wessex, and there is evidence of a raid in

---

[3] English Heritage. (2023, August 10). *Early Christianity in Anglo-Saxon Northumbria.* Retrieved from English-heritage.org.uk: https://www.english-heritage.org.uk/visit/places/lindisfarne-priory/History/.

Kent around 753 CE. However, the raid on Lindisfarne was much more significant. The monastery was more than an isolated cloister. Lindisfarne had grown into an economic and political powerhouse in Northumbria. There were as many as four hundred people living on the island, which made it a huge community. The monastery had extensive landholdings. Moreover, the Vikings probably had a good idea of what Lindisfarne had as far as treasure. There is evidence that merchants from Scandinavia had been trading up and down the coast of Northumbria for years by 793.

The raid took place on June 8th, 793 CE. The *Anglo-Saxon Chronicle*, written sometime in the late 9th century, was succinct in its description: "The woeful inroads of heathen men destroyed God's church in Lindisfarne island by fierce robbery and slaughter."

That account would later be elaborated on by Symeon of Durham, whose account was a little more dramatic:

"They [the Vikings] miserably ravaged and pillaged everything. They trod the holy things under their polluted feet, they dug down the altars, and plundered all the treasures of the church. Some of the brethren they slew, some they carried off with them in chains, the greater number they stripped naked, insulted, and cast out of doors, and some they drowned in the sea."

The Shocking News

It was the reaction of the rest of Europe that made the raid on Lindisfarne so prominent. Charlemagne's court received the news, and Alcuin, Charlemagne's primary advisor, expressed genuine horror over what had happened.

The raid of Lindisfarne is considered the start of the Viking Age. Although the monastery survived for nearly one hundred years afterward, everything had changed. The entire coast of England was exposed to danger. Every monastery or undefended town was liable to be a victim of the Northmen.[4]

---

[4] Marsh, A. (2022, June 21). *In 793 AD, Vikings attacked Lindisfarne. Here's why it was so shocking.* Retrieved from National Geographic.co.uk:
https://www.nationalgeographic.co.uk/history-and-civilisation/2022/06/in-793ad-vikings-attacked-lindisfarne-heres-why-it-was-so-shocking.

A Nasty Surprise

The attack on Lindisfarne was likely not a major assault; no more than four ships and a combined force of one hundred men attacked. The surprise factor was what gave the Vikings the advantage. Historians have suggested that the monks possibly did not know what was going on until they saw drawn swords. By then, it was too late to do anything but beg for mercy.

What makes the raid more shocking is that Scandinavian traders had been working up and down the coast and into the English Channel for years. There was no way to identify a trading ship from a Viking raider at that point, so no one could tell if the ship on the horizon was a Viking vessel. It came down to whom one could trust off the shores of England.

Prizes to Be Had

In any event, the Vikings began to target the wealthy monasteries along the coast. These English monasteries were rich in gold, silver, and other valuable goods, and they proved an irresistible target for the raiders. There would be an attack on the Benedictine abbey at Jarrow the following year and an assault on Iona the year after that. The assault on Jarrow was repulsed, but it did not stop later attacks on the monastery or on Lindisfarne.

The monks who lived in these monasteries were easy targets since they were not trained warriors. They had no weapons and no military training. The Vikings encountered little to no resistance from them, which led to further raids.

Something else was happening during all these incursions. Viking sailors were getting an idea of the lay of the land. They noticed the agricultural opportunities that were present in England. The raids were not just for the sake of gaining plunder; they were a chance to do some real estate hunting, which would prove valuable a few decades later.

In the Midst of Chaos

The attacks on the English coast might have had very different outcomes if a unified front and a strong coastal defense were present. Unfortunately for the English, that was not possible. What is now modern England was divided into four kingdoms in the 9th century: Northumbria, Mercia, Wessex, and East Anglia. Each had its own set of laws and political agendas. A Viking raid on Northumbria meant nothing to Mercia. In fact, such incursions would be desirable because they would distract Northumbria from trying to dominate other kingdoms.

The same is true for the other kingdoms. An attack on one was not necessarily an attack on all of them. However, the Vikings were not a menace that was going to go away. In fact, as the years progressed, the danger grew significantly worse with every passing year.

There was a serious dynastic rivalry in Northumbria between the royal houses of Deira and Bernicia. It created considerable dissension in England's largest kingdom. Between 737 and 806, Northumbria had ten kings. Five were expelled, three were murdered, and two retired to become monks. The raids on Northumbria's monasteries continued, and in 800, monasteries at Whitby, Tynemouth, and Hartlepool were assaulted. Northumbria's internal problems continued to make it vulnerable to outside attacks.

The developments in Northumbria were no doubt reported back to Scandinavia by traders who did business in England. We can think of them as industrial spies who saw opportunities developing thanks to inner chaos that prevented a strong resistance.[5]

Viking raids intensified in the 9th century. They were no longer small assaults but large-scale incursions. The distress spread to other parts of the island. The Vikings were defeated in 838 and in 851, but that did not stop raids in East Anglia, Kent (which became part of Wessex in 845), Wessex, and Northumbria.[6]

Just as a reminder, some of the accounts of the ferocious Vikings must be taken with a grain of salt. The stories of horror were penned by monks who had a revenge agenda. Their monasteries were burned, and their brother clergy were killed or dragged off to slavery. It is probable that tales of terror were deliberately exaggerated to make Vikings appear to be sons of Satan. They were rough sailors and not to be trifled with, but they most likely did not roast babies for dinner.

The Danes Are Coming!

The Vikings stopped concentrating on Northumbria and made attacks in southern England as well. Denmark was becoming the starting point for increasingly more incursions.

---

[5] England's North East. (203, August 10). *Northumbria's Downfall*. Retrieved from Englandsnortheast.co.uk: https://englandsnortheast.co.uk/northumbria-anarchy/.
[6] Dorothy Whitlock, W. A. (2023, August 10). *The Period of the Scandinavian Invasions*. Retrieved from Britannica.com: https://www.britannica.com/place/United-Kingdom/The-church-and-the-monastic-revival.

Plunder was not the only reason for Danish Vikings to have an interest in England. Danish society had a high regard for martial prowess and bravery. An ordinary warrior could gain a great deal of prestige and honor if he came back with considerable spoils. That man might even be named in one of the Viking sagas and oral traditions, guaranteeing that he would be remembered long after he was dead.

Denmark was also experiencing overpopulation. There was not enough arable land, and there were too many mouths to feed. The possibility of finding extensive tracts of farmland made England appealing as a place for future settlement.

Society in Denmark was full of feuds and duels fought because of honor. The chance to send aggressive men who could be troublemakers on long sea voyages would ensure that things remained quiet in the region as long as they were gone.

The slave trade needs to be thought of as a reason for striking England as well. Slavery was a part of Scandinavian culture, and victims of a Viking raid could be taken back as slaves. A chance to establish trade networks or take over existing ones was a possible reason as well.

The Danes would gradually become an even more potent force in English history as the Viking Age progressed. They were not in this enterprise to just gather up shiny bobbles and jewels.

Wintering in England

Early Viking raids were essentially grab-and-run affairs, but in 850, the *Anglo-Saxon Chronicle* had an interesting entry.

"In this year Ealdorman Ceorl with the contingent of the men of Devon fought against the heathen army at Wicganbeorg, and the English made a great slaughter there and had the victory. And for the first time, heathen men stayed through the winter on Thanet."[7]

This time, the Vikings were not racing home to celebrate or escape. They were wintering in a land they were accustomed to only plundering. The significance of this is subtle, but it is revealing. Vikings were developing an interest in England that went beyond making a quick profit. They were probably starting to consider the area as a possible place for settling down. Migration to England would certainly solve the overpopulation problem back home. Many Vikings were farmers, not

---

[7] History-maps.com. (2023, August 10). *Viking Invasions of England.* Retrieved from History-maps.com: https://history-maps.com/story/Viking-Invasions-of-England.

professional raiders.

Perhaps wintering in England was not out of necessity. The Vikings who stayed there had an opportunity to do some very detailed scouting and information gathering. The intelligence they brought back to Scandinavia would have influenced the decisions of very powerful men. The outcome of this stay would be realized several years later when the raids became something more than a plundering visit.

Primary Actors

The Viking Age provided history with a colorful cast of characters. Some of their exploits may appear a bit fanciful, but their individual contributions are too great to ignore. Here are some of the prominent players.

Famous Vikings

- Rollo of Normandy was so successful in his raids on France that he was finally given land at the mouth of the Seine in exchange for converting to Christianity and promising not to raid again. The land he ruled would become known as Normandy.
- Sweyn Forkbeard was, at one point, the king of England, Denmark, and parts of Norway. He will receive more attention later in this book.
- Gunnar Hamundarson was an Icelandic chief who was known for his fighting ability and athletic prowess. It was said that he was able to jump his own height!
- Erik the Red was another Icelander, and his claim to fame was discovering Greenland. Erik deliberately named the island to convince other Vikings to settle there.
- Leif Eriksson was the son of Erik the Red and was another Viking explorer. He is believed to be the first European to land on the shores of America.
- Cnut, also known as Canute, was the ruler of a great Viking empire. He receives individual attention in this book.[8]

Famous Anglo-Saxons

The Kingdom of Wessex produced the most memorable Anglo-Saxons. They will receive attention later in this book.

---

[8] Warriors and Legends.com. (2023, August 31). *Famous Viking Warriors*. Retrieved from Warriorsandlegends.com: https://www.warriorsandlegends.com/viking-warriors/famous-viking-warriors/.

- Alfred the Great
- Edward the Elder
- Æthelstan

Raids from Denmark were particularly marked from 835 CE onward. The Danish Vikings targeted Northumbria, the most powerful Anglo-Saxon kingdom at the time. They captured York twice in 866 and 873 CE and established their own kingdom there, known as the Kingdom of Jorvik. This kingdom was ruled by the famous Viking warrior Guthrum, who battled against the Anglo-Saxon king, Alfred the Great. Ultimately, however, Guthrum was defeated and forced to sign a peace treaty in 886 CE, which allowed the Vikings to retain control of the Kingdom of Jorvik but on English terms.

Chapter Two: Ragnar Lothbrok

The History Channel series *Vikings* features a notorious Viking named Ragnar Lothbrok (also spelled as Ragnar Lodbrok). According to Viking lore, Ragnar was the son of a hero, Sigurd Hring, and his wife, Alfhild. He was a man of legend and is credited with being a highly successful raider of England and other parts of Britain and perhaps even Ireland. His story is a combination of fact and fiction.

Viking oral histories and sagas are not always factually correct. They are often highly exaggerated accounts of the deeds of men, who are made to appear almost superhuman. One reason for this is that the storytellers were stressing the fame and power of the individual. Another problem is that hundreds of years often passed before the accounts were recorded. The primary source of information we have for Ragnar Lothbrok is the *Ragnarssona pattr* (the *Tale of Ragnar's Sons*). Other places where Ragnar is mentioned include *Gesta Danorum* (*Deeds of the Danes*), a Danish document that is reasonably accurate, and the *Anglo-Saxon Chronicle*.

It has been suggested that the accounts of Ragnar were deliberately exaggerated to make him look like a more significant threat than he actually was. The intent was to make him look so ferocious and terrifying that just mentioning his name could spread fear among his enemies.[9]

---

[9] Irvine, A. (2022, December). *10 Facts About Viking Warrior Ragnar Lodbrok.* Retrieved from Historyhit.com: https://www.historyhit.com/facts-about-viking-ragnar-lodbrok/.

His Raiding Resume

Vikings suggests that Ragnar led the raid on Lindisfarne in the 8th century. This is not true because Ragnar was not yet born when the attack happened.

Ragnar had a reputation for being a great warrior and became wealthy due to raids on vulnerable territories. Icelandic sources that have been somewhat verified by the Anglo-Saxons tell of a ferocious Viking named Ragnall who terrorized northeastern England. He might have been Ragnar.[10]

Viking lore implies that Ragnar attacked Paris around 845. It was assumed that he commanded a fleet of 120 Viking ships, which means that he went after Paris with six thousand men. That was a sizable army in those days.

A 19th-century depiction of Vikings attacking Paris.
https://commons.wikimedia.org/wiki/File:Viking_Siege_of_Paris.jpg

But was it even remotely possible that Ragnar could do this? Yes. There was also a later attack on Paris that took place in 885. This was the most significant Viking raid on the city. The initial estimate is that the

---

[10] The Ministry of History. (2020, May 5). *Ragnar Lothbrok*. Retrieved from Theministryofhistory.co.uk: https://www.theministryofhistory.co.uk/historical-biographies/ragnarlothbrok.

Viking force had three hundred to seven hundred ships with anywhere from thirty thousand to forty thousand men. That estimate is a gross exaggeration. Historian John Norris estimates that the Viking force was around three hundred vessels, meaning the Viking army was approximately fifteen thousand men. That is still a significant army in the 9th century.

We need to keep in mind that this type of attack was possible thanks to the longships. Their shallow draft permitted them to go upriver instead of landing forces on the seashore. The sight of the Viking armada heading into the heart of France must have terrified everybody who saw it.

The attack of 885 was unsuccessful. Although the French were able to block the passage of the Viking ships down the Seine, the raiders were not deterred. The Vikings were able to retreat by dragging their boats overland to the Marne. Before they did that, the Vikings conducted a raid on Burgundy, which is even farther inland. The Vikings' ability to attack targets that were a considerable distance from the coast made people greatly fear them.

Legend has it that Charles the Fat paid a substantial bribe to Ragnar so that he would go away. Ragnar was only too happy to accept the money. Just attacking Paris gave him considerable prestige in the Viking world. Besides, there were other rich targets with weaker defenses. Saxo Grammaticus, a Danish historian who lived from around 1160 to 1220, tells us that Ragnar raided Ireland in 851 and continued his raiding along the Irish coast and northwestern England.[11]

Viking Raiding Tactics

Ragnar made use of a lightning strike tactic to overcome his victims. He demoralized and overwhelmed his opponent before they could gather enough strength to successfully oppose him. Ragnar was also a prudent general. He would fight when the odds were in his favor and would not take unnecessary risks.

Viking military strategy was very flexible. It all depended on the circumstances they were confronted with when they got off the boat.

---

[11] Butler, J. (2023, August 29). *The Real Ragnar Lothbrok*. Retrieved from Histori-uk.com: https://www.historic-uk.com/HistoryUK/HistoryofEngland/Ragnar-Lothbrok/#:~:text=This%20may%20well%20have%20been,settlement%20not%20far%20from%20Dublin.

These men were out for loot, and they wanted to survive the raid. Vikings were quite willing to set up ambushes or engage in sneak attacks if it would help them gain their objective.

One very effective battle tactic the Vikings employed was the "boar's snout." It was meant to break the battle line of an enemy. A wedge of warriors was formed that would attack one part of the enemy line with the intention of breaching the defense. Once the line was broken, the Vikings would take advantage of the ensuing chaos.[12]

Ragnar's success stemmed from a society that nurtured a warrior spirit. Vikings were men who learned to fight early and had a cohesive spirit that encouraged group action. Making a Viking did not happen in a few weeks of basic training. It was a lifestyle born in childhood.

Grooming a Viking

Ragnar had several sons. Three of them, Halfdan, Ivar (known as Ivar the Boneless), and Ubba, would play significant roles in a massive Viking assault that happened in the late 9th century. Ragnar's sons were likely prepared for a life that would be part domestic work and violent action since they were boys.

When we say domestic work, we mean farming and crafts. Vikings were raiders, but Vikings only typically raided for a season. They would then come home to be farmers and craftsmen. A boy needed to learn how to excel in an occupation and be a skilled warrior.

History gives us detailed accounts of how the Spartans trained their boys to become exceptional fighters. We have no Viking training manual, but we can guess that boys learned what to do by working with their fathers and extended families. Uncles, grandfathers, and older brothers would be important teachers and mentors. Historians think that fighting was always part of a boy's training. If a boy was fighting another boy over a silly quarrel, the child was not punished severely unless serious physical harm happened.[13]

Viking sagas mentioned that boys were trained for war. The poem *Rigsthula* describes the education of a boy who could tame horses, shape

---

[12] Curry, A. (2017). *How to Fight Like a Viking*. Retrieved from Nationalgeographic.com: https://www.nationalgeographic.com/history/article/vikings-fight-warfare-battle-weapons.

[13] Legends and Chronicles. (2023, August 20). *Viking Children*. Retrieved from legendsandchronicles.com: https://www.legendsandchronicles.com/ancient-civilizations/the-vikings/viking-children/.

shields, make arrows, and brandish spears. It is possible that toddlers learned how to play with wooden swords. There is evidence that children received real weapons that were suited to the size of the child. Archaeologists in Norway have found an ax and a sword in a minor's grave.

Wrestling was a popular sport in Viking culture, and it taught practical war skills, such as speed and agility. Snowball fights were opportunities to build snow forts and practice different throwing skills. Boys were allowed to play rough, but they were not permitted to hurt anybody. Breaking the rules in the wild and tumble games, committing what was called a *nio*, was a severe juvenile offense. (There is not enough evidence to know if girls were taught to fight, but it is a possibility.)

The Viking culture prized honor above other qualities. A code of honor was instilled into a young boy from the beginning. Bravery was an expected virtue that each boy needed to have because only a brave warrior would be permitted to enter Valhalla.

A grim part of the training was the battle itself. The sagas mentioned cases where a boy as young as nine killed a man. These may be exaggerations, but the understanding in Viking communities was very clear. A young man must be ready to enter battle for honor or pillage. There was no minimum age for combat.

Vikings as Fighters

Ragnar did not go a-roving with a band of amateurs. His crew was comprised of military-minded men who knew what they were doing. All accounts of Vikings from the sagas and the writings of monks indicate that these men were perhaps the best fighters of the Middle Ages. They had superior longships and excellent weapons, and they were trained from early childhood to be fighters. Some unique qualities of the Vikings made them nearly invincible.

- Esprit de Corps

Morale is essential for any fighting force, and raiding Vikings had high levels of confidence. An important reason for this esprit de corps, besides fighting for honor and loot, was the way the crews were comprised. The boat crews were formed from the men who came from the same village or local area. They knew each other from birth and were often relatives or close friends. A raiding expedition would be at sea for weeks to get to and from their destinations. The men got to know each other and developed strong connections.

The notion of a band of shield brothers was critical in a military engagement. No one wanted to look like a coward in front of their neighbors or relatives. Running from a battle would bring shame to a person, and that dishonor would last a lifetime. Like the legendary three hundred Spartans, Vikings would stand together and fight to the last man if necessary. Evidence from excavations of burial sites shows groups of Vikings buried together. It is likely they all fell fighting to defend each other.

- Berserkers

Berserkers are major characters in the stories of the Northmen. They were reportedly half-crazed wild men who would attack without concern for bodily harm and fought until they won or were killed. They were the insane warriors of Scandinavia. That is the mythology behind them. Historians have to go a little bit deeper than the fanciful tales to discover the truth behind these shock forces.

Berserkers traditionally prepared themselves for a fight. They permitted rage to take over, and their bodies would convulse with adrenaline rushes. Growling would indicate that they were ready for battle. However, this might not have been naturally induced.

One theory has it that they would get drunk before fighting. It could be the traditional mead drink or one that had some special herbs mixed into the beverage. Some scholars also believe a berserker was high on hallucinogenic mushrooms. Combining the ingredients of the mushroom with an already elevated state of anger would push the berserker into an uncontrollable rage. There are mushrooms in Scandinavia that do have hallucinogenic attributes.

Stories only embellish the image of these fighters. They reportedly went into battle wearing wolf pelts. They might also have gone into a conflict either naked or without armor. That could make this person dangerous because they had even greater freedom of movement.

One challenge with learning more about the berserker is there is so little physical evidence of them. Nevertheless, the rumor that berserkers were in the ranks of the Viking force would be sufficient to terrify any opponent.[14]

---

[14] Warriors & Legends. (2023, August 20). *Viking Warrior Raids.* Retrieved from Warriorsandlegends.com: https://www.warriorsandlegends.com/viking-warriors/viking-warrior-raids/.

Viking Raiding Parties

Why were people so afraid of Ragnar and the other Vikings? The attack of a Viking longship could be dealt with. A levy of the local militia could easily overcome twenty or thirty people from a boat. There was something more to the raiding parties that struck terror into the hearts of people in England.

To begin with, being attacked by one dragon longship was not the standard method of operation. Professor Kenneth Harrell has estimated that a typical raiding party coming out of Scandinavia would have been as many as ten or twenty ships. When we do the math and calculate the number of vessels by a crew of fifty or sixty armed warriors, that raiding party grows to 500 to 1,200 battle-tested men.

The size of these raids grew over time. Viking incursions in the early 9th century might have seen up to one thousand warriors on twenty ships. That number would expand by the start of the 10th century to as many as one hundred ships and a force of five thousand to twelve thousand warriors. That is not just a simple raiding party; that is an invasion force!

It is estimated that the size of Viking raiding parties grew from three ships in the early 9th century to thirty or more ships by 850. This would mean that in the early days of the Viking Age, the raiding party would be no more than 150 warriors. The size of the strike force would be thirty ships or more by mid-century, and that means an invading force of 850 to 1500 men at arms. The later days of the ninth century might mean that a force of five thousand men would come in on hundreds of vessels.[15]

The English kingdoms were placed on the defensive because of Ragnar and other Vikings. The hit-and-run tactics of the Norsemen were difficult to counter because they were sudden and quick; Vikings were often gone before a relief force could appear on the scene.

The situation in both England and Ireland is best described by a church antiphony of the time: "Our supreme and holy Grace, protecting us and ours, deliver us, God, from the savage race of Northmen which

---

[15] Ulvog, J. (2017, November 8). *Size of Viking raiding parties*. Retrieved from Ancientfinances.com: https://ancientfinances.com/2017/11/08/size-of-viking-raiding-parties/#:~:text=In%20The%20Vikings%20course%20from,500%20up%20to%201%2C200%20warriors.

lays waste to our realms."[16]

Ragnar's death was suitably horrible. The *Gesta Danorum* records that King Ælla of Northumbria eventually captured him. We would think that a Viking like Ragnar would be hanged or beheaded, but there was a little theater in the way he was terminated. The king had his prisoner tossed into a pit of venomous snakes.

Ragnar reportedly took his death calmly and made an ominous comment before he perished: "How the little piglets would grunt if they knew how the old boar suffers."

Ragnar was referring to his sons and the revenge they would take on his killers when they learned what happened to him.

His sons would take revenge for the death of their father. These three warriors would sail to England with a substantial force of Danish Vikings. However, this was not going to be a large-scale raiding party. Instead, this was an invasion force that England had never seen before. The Danes did not come to burn down a monastery or pillage a village. Their intention was to stay, and the army led by Ragnar's sons was the most dangerous collection of men England had seen in hundreds of years.

---

[16] The Viking Answer Lady. (2023, August 29). *Origin of the phrase, "A furore Normannorum libera nos, Domine*. Retrieved from The Viking Answer Lady: http://www.vikinganswerlady.com/vikfury.shtml.

Chapter Three: The Great Heathen Army

The Anglo-Saxons should have known that there was something afoot. In 850, the Vikings were wintering in England. Additionally, large-scale Viking activities were happening. The *Anglo-Saxon Chronicle* mentions that 350 Viking ships sailed into the mouth of the Thames and attacked London. The Vikings put the Mercian king to flight and then went into Surrey. The Northmen were apparently not content to just raid along the coast. They were starting to go into the interior.

The Vikings were also being met by stiffer resistance than they had seen in the past. In 851, Æthelwulf fought a battle with the Vikings at Aclea and beat them. Another British victory occurred at Sandwich in 851 when King Æthelstan took on a Viking fleet and beat it. The conditions that had made Viking raids so successful in the past were starting to disappear. It was time for the Vikings to use a new tactic, one that would put them at greater risk but would also generate substantial rewards.

Viking raiders and traders were constantly bringing information back home to Scandinavia. There were still internal problems in Northumbria, and internal squabbling between the kingdoms was taking the focus away from dealing with larger threats. Moreover, the English kingdoms were becoming accustomed to paying off the Vikings. A tribute, which was a bribe more than anything else, seemed to be having a positive effect, making the Viking incursions a manageable threat.

A coordinated assault on England could produce substantial gains. It would require a major force to hit the British island and a military campaign that had tangible objectives. This sudden attack would throw the Anglo-Saxon kingdoms off balance and enable Viking raiders to penetrate deep into the countryside.

The idea of the Great Heathen Army probably originated in one of the drinking halls in Denmark. It would be a sustained effort to ravage England.

Origins of the Great Heathen Army

The story of this military force is complex, and there are conflicting stories. It appears that the desire to avenge Ragnar's death was the main reason for the formation of the army.

The Great Heathen Army was a coalition of Vikings from all over Scandinavia. The size of the army is estimated to have been between one thousand and three thousand men.

The force had a great banner under which they fought. It was called *hrafnsmerki*, and it depicted a raven flying upward.

Historians agree that the ultimate goal of this force was the domination of England. It is true that they were still looking for booty, but England was now more than just a raiding target. The Vikings were looking to take land in addition to treasure. England was looked at as a possible place to relocate families, settle down, and create a society with a Norse flavor to it. Each of the major kingdoms of the island would feel the fury of this force.[17]

The Viking Leaders

Ragnar Lothbrok had three sons who would become the leaders of the Great Heathen Army.

- Halfdan Ragnarsson

Halfdan is mentioned in Norse sagas as one of the six sons of Ragnar Lothbrok. He was a leader of the Great Heathen Army and is thought to have been the first Viking king of Northumbria. When the Great Heathen Army split, Halfdan led half of the army north into Northumbria and in attacks on Ireland. He also led his group against the

---

[17] Kruljac, I. (2022, August 20). *The Great Heathen Army: What was it, and how did it unite the Vikings?* Retrieved from Thevikingherald.com: https://thevikingherald.com/article/the-great-heathen-army-what-was-it-and-how-did-it-unite-the-vikings/76.

Picts of Scotland and the Scottish Kingdom of Strathclyde. Halfdan was reportedly killed at the Battle of Strangford Lough while trying to assert his claim to be king of Dublin.

The principal historical source for Halfdan is the *Annals of Ulster*. Coins minted in London in 872 and 873 have his name stamped on them and identify Halfdan as a leader of the Great Heathen Army.

- Ivar the Boneless

Ivar's name is rather unique. Some say it was a result of a curse. It might have been a genetic condition or possibly a mistranslation of an earlier text. We do not know the full story of why he was called the "Boneless." It might not have even been a physical condition at all. We know that Ivar was a very active Viking chief, and he was known for devastating raids. He was also a believer in brutal punishment, including the blood eagle, for anyone who crossed him.

Some stories claim that Ivar was a berserker who was driven by bloodlust. It is generally believed that he was very cunning and intelligent. He was also considered a very skilled tactician. While he was involved with the Great Heathen Army's invasion of England, Ivar is known for his later expeditions in Ireland.[18]

- Ubba

Scholars know the least about Ubba. He is mentioned in the *Passio sancti Eadmundi* as the man who killed King Edmund of East Anglia. He is also accused of having killed an abbess, Aebbe.[19]

Ragnar's sons were infuriated when they found out that their father had been killed. They attacked Northumbria and captured the Northumbrian king, Ælla. To avenge their father, they tortured their prisoner and used the blood eagle method to finish him off. (The blood eagle method required cutting open the victim's back and pulling their ribs and lungs out from behind.) Scholars are not certain this actually happened, but it makes for an amazing story and indicates how savage

---

[18] Sky History. (2023, August 20). *11 Facts About Fearsome Viking "Ivar the Boneless."* Retrieved from History.co.uk: https://www.history.co.uk/articles/11-facts-about-fearsome-viking-ivar-the-boneless.

[19] Williamson, J. (2022, August 20). *Who was Ubba Ragnarsson, the Viking commander of the Great Heathen Army?* Retrieved from Thevikingherald.com: https://thevikingherald.com/article/who-was-ubba-ragnarsson-the-viking-commander-of-the-great-heathen-army/194.

the Vikings could be when seeking revenge.[20]

The Initial Assault

The Great Heathen Army moved forward in 865. They already had a winter camp at Thanet, and they moved from there into East Anglia. The Anglo-Saxon Chronicle records the initial attack.

"This year sat the heathen army in the Isle of Thanet, and made peace with the men of Kent, who promised money therewith; but under the security of peace and the promise of money, the army in the night stole up the country and overran all Kent eastward."

There is an element of treachery in this. The Vikings were promised Danegeld, which was the customary way of solving the problem, but the raiders would not be satisfied with only that. Unbeknownst to the East Anglians, the Danes had bigger objectives in mind, and a few coffers of gold would not be sufficient.

King Edmund

History has been fairly kind to Edmund, King of East Anglia. He is portrayed as a pious man who was not moved by flattery. He would later be canonized and was one of the original patron saints of England.

It appears that King Edmund believed that tribute would get the Vikings out of his kingdom and allow them to go someplace else to do their mischief. It is reported that he gave the Great Heathen Army something they wanted more than gold: horses.

Given the objectives of the Vikings, it makes perfect sense that they would want horses more than gold coins. An army marching on foot takes time to get from one place to another. Marching through territory gives the occupants sufficient time to rally forces and strike back. Horses allow for speed. They can cover ground faster and enhance the element of surprise.

Edmund possibly thought that if he gave the Vikings the horses, they would trot off and bother somebody else. He no doubt figured that if he got them out of East Anglia, his troubles would be over. Time would show that Edmund made a horrible mistake and would pay for it dearly. The Vikings had the mounts they needed to move to the next objective.[21]

---

[20] Sky History. (2023, August 20). *11 Facts About Fearsome Viking "Ivar the Boneless."*

[21] Bishop, C. (2021, March 18). *Horses in battle at the time of Alfred the Great.* Retrieved from Historiamag.com: https://www.historiamag.com/horses-in-battle-at-the-time-of-alfred-the-

Invasion of Northumbria

The Vikings knew the civil war in Northumbria had weakened the kingdom's ability to resist any incursion. Moreover, there was a score that needed to be settled with a certain king.

The Great Heathen Army wintered in Thetford and, in 866, made an ambitious advance across the Humber River into Northumbria. The destination was the city of York. This was a prosperous city and a prize worth taking. The *Anglo-Saxon Chronicle* records what the Danes did:

"The army went from the East-Angles over the mouth of the Humber to the Northumbrians, as far as York. There was an immense slaughter of the Northumbrians, some within and some without; and both the kings were slain on the spot. The survivors made peace with the army."

Despite the defenses of its Roman walls, York fell to Ivar the Boneless in 866, and the name of the city was changed to Jorvik.

Although it has been more than one thousand years since the Vikings were in the area, there are memories of the Northmen in the city. The best known is the suffix "gate," which is given to many streets in modern-day York. It comes from the Viking word *gata*, meaning "street."[22]

The Northumbrians rallied and made an attempt to retake York. Unfortunately, they failed miserably. On March 23rd, 867, Earl Osberht, a claimant to the throne, was killed, and King Ælla was captured and supposedly tortured to death. The two principal leaders of Northumbria had been killed. The Vikings installed a new king, Ecgberht, as a sovereign. He was a puppet, and his only function was to hold down the fort and collect taxes for the Vikings, who were now looking for another prize to plunder.

---

great/#:~:text=King%20Edmund%20of%20East%20Anglia,of%20the%20horses%20they%20needed.

[22] Britain Express. (2023, August 20). *Viking York*. Retrieved from Britainexpress.com: https://www.britainexpress.com/cities/york/viking.htm.

Mercia's Turn

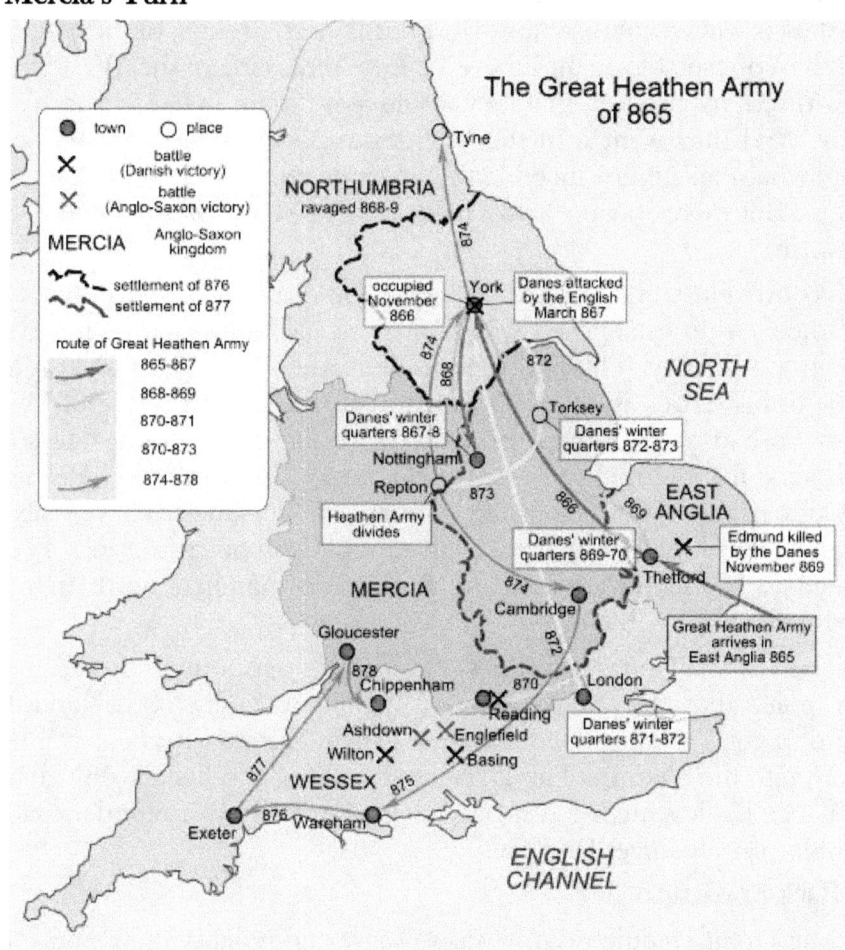

The routes the Great Heathen Army took.
Hel-hama, CC BY-SA 3.0 <https://creativecommons.org/licenses/by-sa/3.0>, via Wikimedia Commons; https://commons.wikimedia.org/wiki/File:England_Great_Army_map.svg

A map of the Great Heathen Army's progress shows that the Vikings crossed Mercia to get to York. It appears strange that the Mercians did not mount a fierce resistance at that time, but they might have been under the misapprehension that all the Vikings were going to do was raid Northumbria and go home. Once again, an Anglo-Saxon kingdom made a terrible mistake. The *Anglo-Saxon Chronicle* continued its story of what the Great Heathen Army was doing. The tale starts with the winter quartering in 867/68.

"This year the same army went into Mercia to Nottingham, and there fixed their winter quarters; and Burhred [Burgred], king of the Mercians, with his counsel, besought Ethered [Æthelred], king of the West-Saxons, and Alfred, his brother; that they would assist them in fighting against the army. And they went with the West-Saxon army into Mercia as far as Nottingham and there meeting the army on the works, they beset them within. But there was no heavy fight; for the Mercians made peace with the army."

To provide some context to the *Anglo-Saxon Chronicle*, the Great Heathen Army established winter quarters at Nottingham, and Mercia was in a quandary. This was the moment when one of the British kings came to his senses about the Viking threat. Burgred, the king of Mercia, knew he had to get help in order to drive the invaders out. He sought assistance from Æthelred. The *Anglo-Saxon Chronicle* refers to him as the king of the West Saxons, which means they came from Wessex, the Anglo-Saxon kingdom that took up most of southern England. Wessex agreed to help Mercia, and an allied force marched north to retake Nottingham.

The city was under siege, and the Vikings were outnumbered. It is at this point that the Anglo-Saxons' inability to fully understand their enemy's goals handicapped their resistance. Burgred negotiated a peace treaty with the Vikings. The Danes were allowed to keep Nottingham in exchange for leaving the rest of Mercia alone. It was a blunder that had terrible consequences later on.[23]

Back to East Anglia

The Great Heathen Army was not just one military unit. There were several forces, each under the command of one of Ragnar's sons. Peace was established in Mercia, and the Vikings looked for someplace else to attack. They fixed their eyes on East Anglia.

This was when it became clear that Edmund had made a terrible misjudgment a few years earlier. He was able to secure peace for his kingdom but only for a brief amount of time. A more prudent sovereign would have recognized that the alliance between Mercia and Wessex meant that the Vikings were more than just a bunch of raiders and pirates.

---

[23] English Monarchs. (2023, August 20). *The Danelaw*. Retrieved from Englishmonarchs.com: https://www.englishmonarchs.co.uk/vikings_11.html

Unfortunately, Edmund underestimated his enemy, and the *Anglo-Saxon Chronicle* tells the story of what happened in East Anglia in 869:

"This year the army rode over Mercia into East-Anglia, and there fixed their winter-quarters at Thetford. And in the winter King Edmund fought with them; but the Danes gained the victory, and slew the king; whereupon they overran all that land, and destroyed all the monasteries to which they came. The names of the leaders who slew the king were Hingwar and Hubba."[24]

Edmund died a vicious death, but we need to be objective about the facts in this matter. East Anglia was defeated in battle, and Edmund was captured. Ivar the Boneless offered to allow Edmund to live if he would renounce his Christian faith. The devout Christian that he was, Edmund refused. The Viking leader then ordered Edmund to be tied to a tree. The East Anglian king was first beaten with cudgels and then whipped. It is believed that Edmund continued to call upon the name of Jesus Christ throughout all of this torture. Ivar was exasperated by the show of piety, and he allowed his troops to use Edmund for target practice. The story has it that Edmund's body looked like that of a porcupine after the target practice was finished. His head was then cut off.[25]

Edmund became Saint Edmund, and a cult of devotion to the martyr developed. He represented a fierce Christian resistance to the heathen Vikings, and he was venerated up until the 16th century. Nevertheless, we have to look at this man with critical eyes. Edmund gave the Vikings the horses they needed to rapidly advance into the middle of England. It appears that he was more concerned with getting the marauders out of East Anglia and did not realize what the long-term consequences of his decision would be. He paid a terrible price for his mistake, but he was not the only monarch who made a bad decision when dealing with the Vikings. Ultimately, only one of the kings of England had a fair assessment of the danger, and he was the one who would vanquish the Great Heathen Army.

---

[24] Medieval Archives. (2020, November 20). *King Edmund the Martyr Killed by the Great Heathen Army.* Retrieved from Medievalarchives.com:
https://medievalarchives.com/2020/11/20/king-edmund-the-martyr-killed-by-the-great-heathen-army/.

[25] New Advent. (2023, August 20). *St. Edmund the Martyr.* Retrieved from Newadvent.org:
https://www.newadvent.org/cathen/05295a.htm.

The Vikings met with success after success in five years. Northumbria became a puppet state, Mercia paid Danegeld to keep the peace, and East Anglia was devastated. Norse immigrants were beginning to settle in the areas that the Great Heathen Army subjugated.

Ivar the Boneless took time off from the English raids. He partnered up with Olaf the White, a Norse king in Ireland, and together, they raided Scotland and sacked Dumbarton.[26]

Looking South to Wessex

There was only one kingdom left for the Vikings to subjugate, and that was Wessex. The morale of the Great Heathen Army was no doubt very high, but it might have gained too much overconfidence.

Wessex was one of the seven major Anglo-Sason kingdoms of the Heptarchy (East Anglia, Mercia, Northumbria, Wessex, Sussex, Essex, and Kent). Wessex would eventually absorb Sussex and be the primary power in southern and southwestern England.

It would prove to be a tough nut to crack, and its rulers were not the type of people who gave up easily. The campaigns in the south would be very different.

Wessex was blessed with advantages its neighbors lacked. It had a strong economy that was centered on agriculture, with some tin mining thrown into the mix. Unlike Northumbria at the time, Wessex was not racked by internal civil war or aristocratic bickering. Unlike East Anglia, it was not ruled by an overly pious person who could not see potential danger. Wessex economy and a stable ruling class gave southern England a better chance of dealing with the Great Heathen Army.

The king of Wessex at the time was Æthelred. He was the son of Æthelwulf and became king in 865 when he was only around twenty years old after his older brother, Æthelberht, had died. The new king was faced with having to deal with the Great Heathen Army and the severe threat to his kingdom.

Æthelred was not intimidated by the Vikings, and he was not about to pay the invaders a bribe. He allied with the Mercians and helped his neighbor try to retake Nottingham. That effort failed, and the Mercians were forced to sue for peace. However, Æthelred was undeterred. He was prepared to continue resisting the Great Heathen Army despite

---

[26] Lewis, R. (2023, August 20). *Ivar the Boneless.* Retrieved from Brittanica.com: https://www.britannica.com/biography/Ivar-the-Boneless.

having to do it alone.

The Invasion of Wessex

The Vikings decided that Wessex would be their next victim, and they launched an assault on that kingdom at the end of 870. Æthelred and his brother Alfred were defeated at Reading, but a few days later, they won a victory at the Battle of Ashdown. The West Saxons lost at Basing and Meretun, but Æthelred still had an army in the field. He was going to need it shortly.

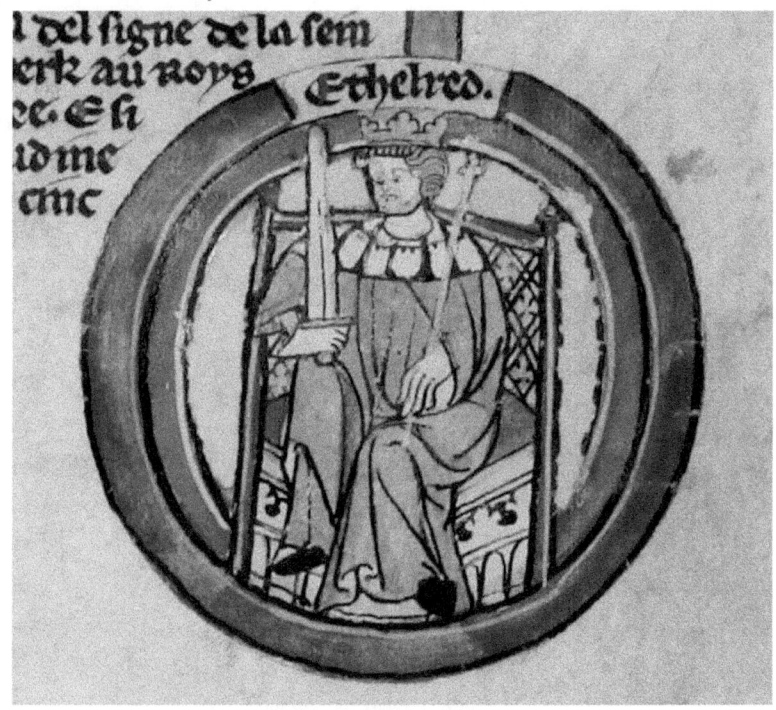

An illustration of Æthelred.
https://commons.wikimedia.org/wiki/File:%C3%86thelred_-_MS_Royal_14_B_VI.jpg

The Vikings received reinforcements from the Great Summer Army, which was commanded by Guthrum, who was a nephew of the Danish king. These troops arrived in April 871 and joined the rest of the Vikings at Reading. Æthelred died shortly after Easter in 871 and was succeeded by his younger brother Alfred. The story of Alfred and the Great Heathen Army will be discussed in greater detail in the following chapters. Suffice it to say for now, Alfred was up against an enormous obstacle.

The Great Heathen Army totally disrupted any sense of order in England. Three of the four kingdoms were devastated, and the damage done to the economy was substantial. The best lesson to be drawn from the experience was the penalty to be paid for lacking a united front.

Northumbria, Mercia, East Anglia, and Wessex might have stopped the Viking incursion in its early stages had they been united in an alliance against the seafaring foe. They were not, and as one kingdom collapsed, the others were desperately trying to find a way to placate the Danes. Only Wessex appreciated the risk of having a foreign army deep in the heart of England. As a result, they faced the Great Heathen Army, knowing that the existence of their kingdom was on the line. No bribe or tribute was going to stop the enemy from obtaining its ultimate goal of complete conquest.

The history of England was turning to a darker page. There seemed to be nothing that could stop the Great Heathen Army. It was at this time in English history that a man stepped forward to confront the foe. All accounts admit he was a great man.

Chapter Four: Alfred the Great

To date, Alfred was the only English monarch to have "the Great" placed after his name. When anyone looks at what Alfred accomplished during his life, that person can immediately recognize why that is so. Alfred justifiably earned that honor, and his reputation is based on facts, not legends.

English history has instances where a person of courage and audacity, such as Elizabeth I or Winston Churchill, stepped forward to lead the nation in a time of crisis. Alfred was one of those who prevented England from spiraling into an abyss. He became the king of Wessex when an epoch in English history might have ended in a cataclysmic disaster.

Alfred was the son of Æthelwulf and his wife, Osburh. The old king had five sons, and four of them would go on to rule over Wessex. The Wessex line of succession shows a peaceful transfer from one brother to another since most of the brothers did not have heirs. There is also evidence that a brother would help his ruling sibling in times of danger. This might be one of the reasons why the Kingdom of Wessex had a stable monarchy and a society that was not prone to civil war.

Accession to Power

Alfred provided assistance to his brother during the fierce resistance against the incursions of the Great Heathen Army into Wessex. However, Æthelred died, leaving behind infant sons. The kingdom was in a severe predicament and could not afford to have a child on the throne. Alfred had an understanding of the dangers Wessex faced, having been on the front lines of the resistance from the beginning of the Great Heathen Army's invasion in 865. The country's ruling class decided to bypass the small children and give Alfred the crown.

The Vikings now controlled the eastern half of England. Having beaten or cowed the other three Anglo-Saxon kingdoms, the foreign army was now able to turn all of its resources and might against the southern kingdom.

Alfred continued the fight, but he was facing an adversary that was relentless. He was faced with no other alternative but to find a way to buy peace. Fortunately for him, the Viking commanders, Guthrum and Halfdan, were willing to listen to his terms.

It is not that surprising that the Vikings were amenable to negotiation. They had been fighting for over six years and had suffered losses. Their casualties were high, and morale was starting to sink. The opportunities for plunder were vanishing, and there was a growing desire in the ranks to settle their families in the newly conquered lands. Nevertheless, the price for peace was going to be stiff.

Alfred was required to pay an annual payment of Danegeld and cede eastern England to the Vikings. This meant that, by 873, the Vikings had control of East Anglia, Northumbria, Mercia, and the eastern section of Wessex. Alfred was willing to concede to the conditions. The Wessex king realized he had to buy time to make a stand.[27]

Viking Worries

The Great Heathen Army had wintered in late 871, no doubt welcoming the rest from the ongoing fighting. Their leaders needed to reassess their priorities and determine their next moves. Halfdan noticed some problems were occurring in the north. The Northumbrians had been defeated, but that did not mean they were satisfied with their new overlords. There was a rebellion against Ecgberht that needed to be suppressed. The Mercians paid the Danegeld to keep the peace, but there were problems underneath the surface. In 873, Ivar the Boneless died. Halfdan lost a valuable war chief.

Burgred was going to learn that paying off the Vikings didn't guarantee security for his throne. The Great Heathen Army attacked

---

[27] MacNeil, R. (2019, May). *The Great Heathen Failure: Why the Great Heathen Army Failed to Conquer the Whole of Anglo-Saxon England*. Retrieved from Digitalcommons.winthrop.edu: https://digitalcommons.winthrop.edu/cgi/viewcontent.cgi?article=1105&context=graduatetheses.

Mercia in 874, and Burgard was forced to flee for his life. He eventually went into exile in Rome and died there. The Vikings now had complete control over Mercia.[28]

It was apparent to the Viking commanders that there was nothing more to accomplish as a united force. In addition, Northumbria and Mercia needed to be watched, and any possible rebellions had to be put down. It was a time when permanent residence in England was the new Viking priority.

In 874, the Great Heathen Army divided. Halfdan went north and began the process of settling his men in the lands they had conquered. Guthrum remained behind with his portion of the army. Although Alfred would facie Guthrum in the coming years, he would be confronting a much smaller enemy force.[29]

The Wessex Campaign

Peace did not mean that Alfred was enjoying the quiet. He used this time to reestablish his authority in Wessex and recruit an army. Unlike his fellow Anglo-Saxon kings, Alfred did not trust the Vikings to honor the peace or remain inactive. He kept an army ready for any new outbreak of war. It was a very smart strategy.

Guthrum attacked in 875. He was using a course of action that succeeded in the past: occupying a town and waiting for a chance to receive money in return for a promise to leave. They did this in Wareham. Alfred was not able to take Wareham and negotiated a peace treaty with Guthrum. The Vikings promptly broke their word and killed the hostages that Alfred had provided. They moved into Exeter, where Alfred successfully blockaded the Viking ships. The Vikings negotiated a peace with Alfred in late 877 and retreated to Gloucester. However, they still kept their goal of gaining control over all of Wessex.

Alfred wintered in Chippenham for Christmas in 877. The Danes attacked Alfred in January 878 and forced Alfred to flee with a small group of men into the wilderness. The Vikings had the upper hand, but they did not have the king.

---

[28] Discovery. (2023, May 3). *Who was King Burgred of Mercia and what did he do?* Retrieved from Discoveryuk.com: https://www.discoveryuk.com/monarchs-and-rulers/who-was-king-burgred-of-mercia-and-what-did-he-do/.

[29] MacNeil, R. (2019, May). *The Great Heathen Failure: Why the Great Heathen Army Failed to Conquer the Whole of Anglo-Saxon England.*

Some historians criticize Alfred, saying that he was not able to defeat the Danes in open-field combat successfully. He seemed more prone to pay off the Vikings and get them to leave for a while.

After the near disaster at Chippenham, Alfred was a monarch with a barely effective fighting force. Fortunately for Wessex, events were about to change. The year 878 proved to be a very decisive one.

The Burning Cakes

Alfred escaped after nearly being taken prisoner and fled into hiding. He found refuge in the marshes of Somerset and laid low on the Isle of Athelney. Here is where one of the more delightful legends about King Alfred originated.

Alfred was in a small hut. He was asked by the lady of the house to watch over some griddle cakes (small bread loaves). Alfred agreed, but he was so distracted by his worries over what to do that he completely forgot his chore. The cakes burned, and the woman was furious. Legend has it that she scolded and even beat the king of Wessex with a broom. Alfred did not tell her that he was the king and graciously accepted his punishment. The story shows King Alfred to be not just a regal person but also somebody who was fair. He did something wrong, apologized for it, and did not try to punish the lady for her behavior.

There is no way we can check this story's accuracy because there is no record of it from the time. Actually, it was not mentioned at all until several hundred years after it supposedly took place. Nevertheless, it depicts a man who was willing to accept punishment, and it enhances the legend of Alfred the Great.[30]

The Battle of Edington

Alfred knew he had to strike back and hit the invaders as hard as possible. He waited until the spring of 878 and then sent out a call to his army to assemble at a place known as Egbert's Stone. Once the troops had assembled, Alfred marched them to Edington. There, at some point between May 6th and May 12th, 878, Alfred and his army fought an engagement with the Danes. Alfred's soldiers formed a shield wall and were able to provide stiff resistance. This time, the Danes were beaten. The *Anglo-Saxon Chronicle* gives an account of what happened next.

---

[30] Pearce, S. (2023, February 16). *Where King Alfred Burnt Cakes in Athelney-King Alfred's Monument!* Retrieved from Third Eye Traveler: https://thirdeyetraveller.com/where-king-alfred-burnt-cakes-in-athelney-king-alfreds-monument/.

"He [Alfred] pursued them as far as their fortress [Chippenham] and besieged them therefore fortnight. This time it was the Vikings who had to give in and sue for peace. They gave him hostages and swore great oaths to leave the kingdom, and also that their king would receive baptism."[31]

The Treaty of Wedmore

After the Battle of Edington, Alfred and Guthrum entered into an agreement over the new status quo in England. It defined the boundary between Wessex and the Viking holdings, recognizing all of what is now south and southwestern England as belonging to King Alfred and Wessex.

The significance of this agreement cannot be understated. The Danes realized there was a limit to their territory. The treaty also required Guthrum to agree to be baptized as a Christian.

Guthrum provided hostages who could be immediately killed if he broke the treaty. Historians have noted that this treaty was the beginning of the historical process that ultimately led to a unified Kingdom of England. Alfred won an immense victory through persistence and courage.

However, this did not mean that the problems with the Vikings went away. There were still raids and incursions into Wessex.

Alfred had successfully fought back the Danes, using both his army and fleet. However, he realized there had to be a permanent form of defense against the Danes to ultimately discourage them from ever trying to successfully raid his territory.

The Burgh System

Alfred developed a defensive policy that centered on creating fortified towns known as burghs. The basic plan was simple. People were encouraged to settle within these towns in exchange for free plots of land. This created a system of fortified places no more than twenty miles from a town. A Viking raiding party would be within a day's march of a local militia. The burghs also gave farmers a place to find protection.

Alfred enhanced the defensive posture of the burghs by building roads that interconnected them. The Vikings were now in a situation

---

[31] Anglo-Saxon.net. (2023, August 21). *Early-Medieval-England.net Timeline: 871-899*. Retrieved from Anglo-Saxon.net: http://www.anglo-saxons.net/hwaet/?do=seek&query=871-899.

where they might be cut off from any escape if they attacked a place. The Northmen did not like the idea of having too many casualties for no reward, so they had to think twice before they ventured into Wessex.

The roads that connected the burghs were also used for trade and other commerce. Alfred essentially created economic centers within his kingdom that could be used to improve the overall economy.

This plan was extensive. As listed in the Burghal Hidage, an Anglo-Saxon document, more than thirty burghs were created.[32]

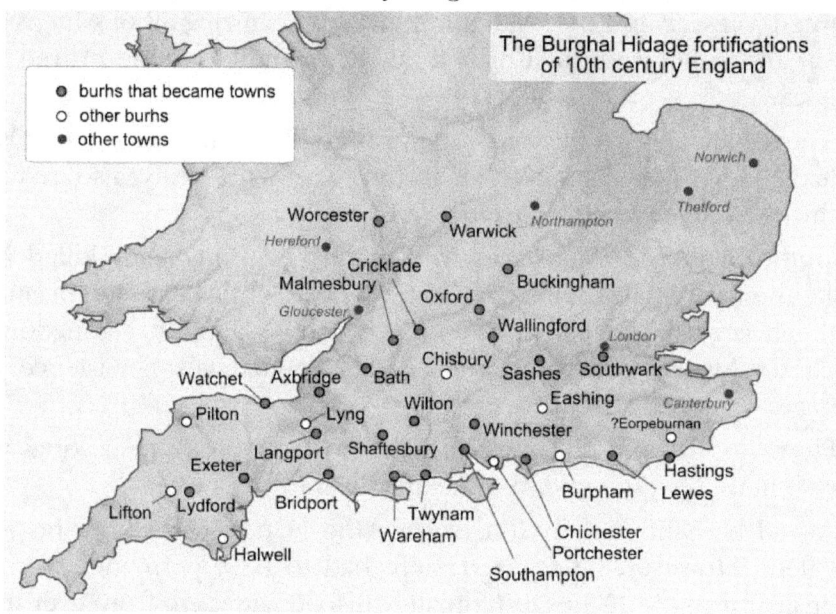

Map of the burghs listed in the Burghal Hidage.
Hel-hama, CC BY-SA 3.0 <https://creativecommons.org/licenses/by-sa/3.0>, via Wikimedia Commons; https://commons.wikimedia.org/wiki/File:Anglo-Saxon_burhs.svg

Further Defenses

The Vikings continued to raid the territory held by King Alfred. A major seaborne attack occurred in 893 that was different than some of the earlier raids. The Vikings brought their families with them with the intention of colonizing. Alfred was able to meet these attacks and outmaneuver his enemies.

---

[32] The History Junkie. (2023, August 21). *5 Reasons That Burhs Were Important and How They Helped Alfred the Great Defeat the Vikings.* Retrieved from Thehistoryjunkie.com: https://thehistoryjunkie.com/5-reasons-that-burhs-were-important-and-how-they-helped-alfred-the-great-defeat-the-vikings/.

One of the changes Alfred made involved sea defense. In 896, he ordered the construction of a small fleet of longships that were each twice the size of a Viking raiding vessel. Although it was not the birth of the English navy, it increased the naval power of Wessex.

Alfred had ships that were swifter, larger, steadier, and rode higher in the water than the Viking boats. He was able to intercept the raiding parties as they were coming across the water, making his kingdom that much safer.

Alfred and Education

Alfred was more than a warrior. He was an innovator and a reformer who brought about significant changes in his kingdom. When he visited Rome, he stayed with Frankish King Charles the Bald and discussed with him how the Carolingian kings were able to deal with the Vikings.

Alfred knew that he needed money to pay for his defenses, so he expanded taxation and based what a person owed on the productivity of that individual's land holdings. A hide was the basic unit for assessing tax obligations. It was the amount of land required to support one's family and would differ in size. Landowners were required to provide services or money based on how many hides that individual owned.

Alfred wanted to create an educational system that would rival the one created by Charlemagne. Court schools were established to educate the nobility and those who were of lower social rank. The curriculum was dedicated to the liberal arts.[33]

Alfred was different from someone who wanted to learn for the sake of learning. He was concerned about the proper execution of justice and sought a better understanding of how to live according to divine principles.

Alfred declared himself king of the Anglo-Saxons in 886. He left behind a kingdom that was in a better situation than when he had found it upon his coronation. His educational reforms, his success in military ventures, and his attempts to preserve the peace and stability of Wessex are all reasons why he is referred to as "Great." We have to admit that his reign was a remarkable period of time in which the character of Anglo-Saxon England was changed for the better.

---

[33] European Royal History. (2022, October 22). *October 26, 899: Death of Alfred the Great, King of the Anglo-Saxons.* Retrieved from Europeanroyalhistory.com: https://europeanroyalhistory.wordpress.com//?s=Alfred+the+Great&search=Go.

It no longer made sense for the Vikings to plunder and destroy the countryside. There was much more to be gained by tilling the fields and engaging in commerce.

Peace was no longer just a pastime to indulge in when the weather was terrible. The Vikings and their families were settling into an area of what is now modern England. It was known as the Danelaw. It lasted for less than one hundred years but left an indelible mark on the English countryside. It is well worth exploring the changes it delivered.

Chapter Five: The Danelaw

The invasion of the Great Heathen Army in 865 was the high watermark of the Viking incursions into England. In the years that followed, the intensity of the Viking attacks began to lessen. There are some primary reasons for the decrease in sea-raiding violence.

Anglo-Saxon communities developed strategies to deal with the marauders. The burgh system established by Alfred the Great created a network of fortified towns that could resist the Vikings, and the local militias were better organized. Alfred's navy could now meet the incoming sea rovers on the open waters. That was a far cry from waiting on the beaches, searching for a dragon longship appearing on the horizon. The Vikings were brave men, but they were not reckless. Attacking a fortified place that was expecting them and ready to inflict severe casualties was too much of a risk.

Guthrum converted to Christianity, and he was not the only Northman to do so. Others accepted the way of the cross, perhaps not always because of a come-to-Jesus moment. Being a Christian offered some possibilities for commercial enterprise, and trade provided more reliable profits than raids. Peaceful activities, such as farming, were tempting alternatives to the slash-and-burn existence of earlier days.

Besides, the Vikings succeeded in their objective of obtaining land in England. Northumbria, Mercia, and East Anglia were under the control of Viking overlords, and the Treaty of Wedmore established fixed boundaries between Wessex and Viking-held land. A new political entity, the Danelaw, came into being.

Creation of a Land of Danes

It was known as *Danelagen* in Danish and *Dena lagu* in Old English. The Danelaw was a recognition that the Vikings were in England to stay. Modern students of history sometimes forget that the Vikings were not just pirates. They were also farmers and exceptional blacksmiths. They had established communities in Scandinavia, and they brought their societies to Anglo-Saxon England. The territory the Vikings inhabited spread from London to East Anglia and through the Midlands up to the north of England.[34]

The significant founding document of the Danelaw was the Treaty of Wedmore. Guthrum had no desire to break the treaty that he had signed, and he was ready to retire from being a marauding nuisance. Danish Mercia was under the control of five Danish armies, which introduced their native laws and customs to this middle section of England. There were five main towns or boroughs established in this Viking-held area: Derby, Leicester, Lincoln, Nottingham, and Stamford. These were all fortified municipalities.

Fifteen shires of modern England would become the Danelaw. These included Leicester, Nottingham, Derby, Lincoln, York, Essex, Cambridge, Suffolk, Northampton, Norfolk, Huntington, Bedford, Middlesex Hertford, and Buckinghamshire.

Important Danelaw Centers

Nottingham was one of the principal towns. The Danish settlement officially started in 877. Derby was settled in 877. The borough of Lincoln was a strategic holding; it was on the route between Wessex and York. Leicester would be the scene of several military engagements while it was part of the Danelaw.[35]

---

[34] Roua, V. (2016, May 7). *A Brief History of the Danish Vikings and of the Danelaw.* Retrieved from Thedockyards.com: https://www.thedockyards.com/the-danish-vikings-and-the-danelaw/.
[35] Brain, J. (2023, August 26). *The Five Boroughs of Danelaw.* Retrieved from Historic-uk.com: https://www.historic-uk.com/HistoryUK/HistoryofEngland/The-Five-Boroughs-Of-Danelaw/.

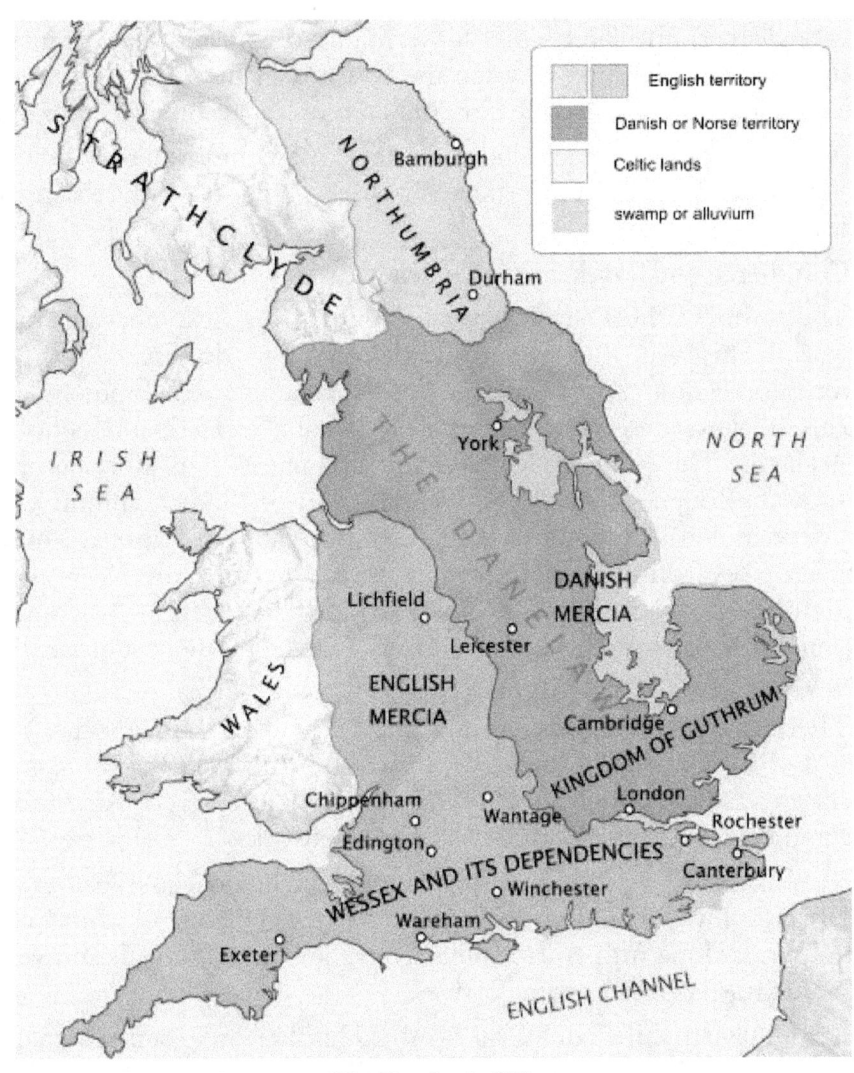

The Danelaw in 878.
Hel-hama, CC BY-SA 3.0 <https://creativecommons.org/licenses/by-sa/3.0>, via Wikimedia Commons; https://commons.wikimedia.org/wiki/File:England_878.svg)

The Population

We do not know precisely how many Scandinavians decided to settle in the Danelaw. While it was an opportunity to expand in a new region, not everybody was willing to leave their old homes for a new place. Only a few thousand might have migrated.

These immigrants intermingled with the Anglo-Saxons. Because of this, a language was created that was a combination of Old Norse and

Old English. Both dialects had a Germanic origin and were similar in many ways. A difference between the two was in the rules of grammar, which could cause some confusion until the two were blended into one.

An Anglo-Norse dialect ultimately developed, and traditional dialects in Yorkshire, Lancashire, the Lake District, and Lincolnshire can trace their roots to this patois.[36]

Commerce and Trade in the Danelaw

The towns of the Danelaw became part of the Scandinavian trading network. This was a commercial highway that dominated northern Europe for centuries and fostered the commercial development of an expanse that covered all of Scandinavia, Britain, Ireland, and as far west as Iceland. The trading towns included places far away as Kyiv, Novgorod, Rouen, Wolin, Dublin, and Truso.[37] The common goods that were traded included slaves, furs, textiles, and iron goods. Imports, such as spices from Byzantium, would enrich the societies that were part of the trade network. Products that had not been seen in Anglo-Saxon England before were being introduced thanks to the extensive trade network.[38]

There were centers of significant trade activity in the Danelaw. York, known as Jorvik to the Danes, was the best example. Excavations in the York area suggest the diversity of goods that entered Anglo-Saxon England because of the Danelaw's trading network.

Manufacturing activities in the Danelaw included glass, leather, and metalwork. Jewelry and dress accessories from Scotland and Ireland were found, along with cowry shells from the Mediterranean and walrus ivory that was imported from Norway.

Scandinavian ships could sail up the Humber and then navigate the Ouse River to York, thanks to the shallow draft of the boats. Trade goods could be taken overland to the west coast and loaded on ships headed for Dublin, Ireland. Other Irish ports included Cork,

---

[36] Viking.no. (2004, August 14). *The Danelaw: Population, culture and heritage.* Retrieved from Viking.no: https://www.viking.no/e/england/danelaw/e-heritage-danelaw.htm.

[37] Skjaden. (2020, January 16). *Trade in the Viking Age-Do You Know Which Trade Towns That Were the Most Important Ones?* Retrieved from Nordic Culture: https://skjalden.com/where-did-the-vikings-trade/.

[38] Skald, F. t. (2016, September 16). *Viking History: Post-by-Post.* Retrieved from Fjorn-the-skald.tumblr.com: https://fjorn-the-skald.tumblr.com/post/150515624715/lesson-16-viking-money-commerce-coins-and.

Waterford, Wexford, and Limerick, which were all trading destinations for Danelaw merchants.

Land travel was possible from York through trails in the valleys. York is situated on a broad, flat plain that stretches south to north and goes through northern England. This meant merchant trade caravans could go north to Scotland or south to Nottingham and Derby.[39]

Law and Administration

The idea of trial by combat and blood feuds makes for exciting television shows, but that is not how affairs were managed in the Danelaw. There was a system of legal practice and administration that permitted society to function in an orderly fashion. The Danelaw's legal system was based on Scandinavian law.

However, the Danelaw's legal practices differed from Anglo-Saxon England. The penalty for killing a person in the Danelaw was determined by a person's social status. Punishments for crimes related to royal jurisdiction in Anglo-Saxon England were significantly harsher, and the spheres of offenses were broader.

The area of the Five Boroughs (Derby, Leicester, Lincoln, Nottingham, and Stamford) had an extensive organization of the judicial system, which included county courts and village court meetings. This system gave rise to the use of juries in English common law. Juries were a feature of Scandinavian jurisprudence, which had previously been unknown in the Anglo-Saxon regions.

The free peasantry, as opposed to serfdom, was a feature of the Danelaw. The idea of a manorial system that relied on feudal ties between a lord and his serfs was not common in the Danelaw. Free farmers were descendants of soldiers and colonists. There was a special category, the sokemen, who were obliged to perform minor duties for their lord, such as paying small rent payments and helping in the fields during harvest. However, these people had complete ownership of their land plots. The relationship with their lord was contractual, not inherited. While the Norman invasion in the 11th century would change things, the sokomen could still be found in East Anglia and the area of the Five Boroughs for centuries.

---

[39] Viking.no. (2004, August 14). *Trade routes in the British Isles.* Retrieved from Viking.no: https://www.viking.no/e/england/york/jorvik_trading_centre_2.html.

The social freedom in the Danelaw led the area to become one of the most prosperous regions of England. Free men turned the forests and wastelands into arable farmland and improved the region's agricultural activity. The innovations and customs that Viking immigrants introduced would serve as models for future English society.[40]

Coinage

A fascinating aspect of the Danelaw's commercial practices was the use of coins. It may seem to be a minor item, but coins permit an economy to make the exchange of goods more manageable. The reason is simple. The alternative would be to use another product or metal bullion to pay for something. It would require either the appraisal of the other trade goods or weight measures to determine how much bullion to pay.

Norsemen originally used a bullion economy and weighed the metal for commercial transactions. The new settlers in the Danelaw were familiar with coins because Danegeld was paid in Anglo-Saxon currency.

Interaction with other foreign trading zones showed the importance of using coins, and in the mid-890s, national coinage was introduced within the Danelaw. Coinage has been found in excavations in York and sites in East Anglia, although not in plentiful numbers. Christian imagery, such as the Christian cross, was commonly found on Danelaw coinage. Bullion was still used, particularly in rural areas, but mints were established in places like York.

---

[40] Chakra, H. (2021, September 27). *The Story of Danelaw*. Retrieved from About-history.com: https://about-history.com/the-story-of-danelaw/.

Examples of Viking coins.
The Portable Antiquities Scheme/ The Trustees of the British Museum, CC BY-SA 4.0 <https://creativecommons.org/licenses/by-sa/4.0>, via Wikimedia Commons; https://commons.wikimedia.org/wiki/File:Thurcaston_Viking_mixed_coin_hoard_(FindID_106146).jpg

Interaction with the Anglo-Saxons

The former sea raiders became more established in England in the 10th century and were involved in diplomacy in the Anglo-Saxon Kingdom of Wessex. Language barriers existed, and they had to be overcome in order to have stable and peaceful relations. As mentioned, Norse words gradually found their way into the developing English language.

Linguistic experts speak of the concept of loanwords. These were infused into English by Old Norse, and it is estimated that around six hundred loaned words are part of today's standard English.

Some of the English words we use every day were derived from Scandinavian sources. Anger, berserk, ransack, and slaughter reflect the age of the Viking raids. Not all of the expressions were violent, though. Sky, skip, happy, and glitter all have origins in Old Norse or

Scandinavian languages.

Days of the week, such as Thursday, came from the Vikings. And some useful words like get, take, and they came from the Northmen.[41]

The Domesday Book, a survey of England completed by William the Conqueror, provides evidence that Scandinavian loanwords were becoming more familiar and were being frequently used. Forty percent of the East Riding of Yorkshire's place names recorded in the Domesday Book have Scandinavian origins. Additionally, 50 percent of the names from Nottingham and Cheshire were Scandinavian. It is argued that this reflects naming conventions, not that there were a large number of Scandinavians in those areas.[42]

Christianity and the Danelaw

Guthrum's conversion was the first significant religious change to affect the new settlers in Anglo-Saxon England. The trend toward Christianity would increase in the 10th century as trade between the Norse and the Anglo-Saxons began to grow. Christianity became a common bond between the Anglo-Saxons and the Danes. Becoming Christian made sense to Norse traders because interactions were much more manageable. It also made Norse settlers more accepted in Anglo-Saxon and European society.

Christianity allowed for a degree of pacification of people who were accustomed to violence. Values such as charity and community service were embraced, and these values, among others, helped in the "domestication" of the sea raiders. There would still be some traces of the Vikings' old customs in folklore and festivals, but Christianity eventually became a fixture in the Danelaw.

The raiders who once burned and pillaged monasteries helped build new ones, and the Archbishopric of York gradually became a vital Christian center in England. An example of Christianity triumphing over the old Norse practices is Oswald of Worcester. He was the archbishop of York from 972 to 992, and he was committed to church reform. Oswald had Danish ancestry and later became a saint.

---

[41] Sky History. (2023, August 26). *Old Norse Words We Use Every Day*. Retrieved from www.history.co.uk: https://www.history.co.uk/shows/vikings/articles/old-norse-words-we-use-every-day.

[42] Fi, B. a. (2015, May 2). *Vikings in the Danelaw*. Retrieved from Babiafi.co.uk: https://www.babiafi.co.uk/2015/05/vikings-in-danelaw.html.

Christianity was also a means of ensuring domestic peace within the Danelaw. Not every inhabitant of the Danelaw was from Scandinavia. Toleration of Christianity made it easier for the Norse overlords to administer their territories and keep the Anglo-Saxon population loyal to them.

Interestingly, cemeteries in Britain give examples of religious integration. There is evidence of pagan burials, and Christian crosses engraved with Scandinavian art have been found on the Isle of Man. The new settlers were willing to incorporate artistic designs with standard Christian imagery.

Guthrum eventually retired to East Anglia and reigned over the Kingdom of Guthrum until his death.

Peaceful relations between the Danes and the Anglo-Saxons did not always last for very long. Friction between the two sides became worse.

The primary difference between the opening years of the 10th century and what had happened before was that the shoe was now on the other foot. The successor of Alfred the Great, Edward the Elder, did not want a potential enemy on his northern border. Aggressive campaigns were fought against the Danes in the Danelaw and in Danish Northumbria. A treaty was signed in 906, but it did not last because Edward harassed the Northumbrian Danes in 909. Edward continued his offensives against the Danes and, by 912, had gained control of the southern Danelaw. The following years saw Edward defeating the Danes in several battles.

Edward the Elder was part of the resurgence of Anglo-Saxon England. The Anglo-Saxons were not as fractious as they had been in earlier years; rather, they were uniting under the king of the Anglo-Saxons.

The downfall of the Danelaw was also caused by internal struggles that drew attention away from the military threat creeping up from the south.

Cultural assimilation weakened the ties with the Norse culture. Intermarriage caused the Scandinavians to lose their distinctive identity as they mingled more and more frequently with Anglo-Saxons. The use of Old English became more frequent, and Christianity strengthened the connections with the Anglo-Saxons.

The Scandinavians were no longer a unique group, and they were facing an enemy that presented a united front against them. It was the

Anglo-Saxons who now desired to have control over the country. The rulers of the Danelaw were increasingly at a disadvantage.

Æthelstan, the son of Edward the Elder, continued the aggressive policy against the Danelaw. The former Vikings were gradually being forced back from their original holdings. Anglo-Saxons benefited from a more organized military strategy and political alliances. The Danelaw ceased to be a political entity in 954 when Eric Bloodaxe was driven out of Northumbria.

The next chapter will take a closer look at how the Danelaw fell.

Chapter Six: Edward and Æthelstan

Any period of sustained peace gave the Anglo-Saxons the opportunity to consolidate their positions and plan future ways of expansion into the territory of the Danelaw. It was obvious that having a foreign power control vast portions of England was not the best foreign policy. The now-settled Vikings had their own legal system, which could not be easily reconciled with existing Anglo-Saxon law. In addition, these foreigners controlled important trade routes and resources, which could impact the economy of the south. Matters were made worse when Vikings attacked Anglo-Saxon territory, acting more like brigands than peaceful neighbors. England was, for all practical purposes, a house divided. That state of affairs could not stand for long.

Edward Ascends to Power

Edward the Elder ruled from 899 to 924. He was the son of Alfred the Great, and he intended to follow in his father's footsteps as much as possible. The reconquest of England south of the Humber was a long-term goal that he pursued.

We do not know much about Edward before he became king. Asser's *Life of King Alfred*, written in 893, says that Edward was an obedient son to Alfred and somebody who treated others with friendliness, humility, and gentleness. Edward was not an ignorant clod. He was well-educated and familiar with books.

What sources we have indicate that Edward was a fighter and a popular person in the royal family. We believe that Alfred gave Edward some degree of independent authority and that the old king appointed Edward as a sub-king of Kent. Edward appeared to be a legitimate and competent successor to his father, but he would have to earn his birthright on the battlefield.

The Æthelwold Revolt

Alfred had other male kin who could make a claim to the throne of Wessex. One of them was his nephew, Æthelwold. He was the son of Alfred's older brother, Æthelred I, and Æthelwold rebelled because he believed that he had as much of a right to the throne as Edward did.

After Edward was crowned king, Æthelwold seized Wimborne in Dorset. Edward forced him to vacate that position, and Æthelwold escaped to Northumbria. There, Danes swore allegiance to him and declared him their king. Æthelwold assembled a fleet and, in late 901, landed his force in Essex. The following year, he persuaded East Anglian Danes to unite with him and began raiding in Wiltshire and Wessex. The final confrontation between Edward and Æthelwold happened in 902 at the Battle of the Holme. Æthelwold. was killed in the fight, which ended any opposition to Edward being king of Wessex.

Æthelwold's rebellion exposed a danger to Edward and his reign. It was more than just a false claimant trying to take his throne; the support of the Danes and the Danelaw was very troubling. Edward could not rest easy with a nation on his borders that could support another rebellion at a later date. There needed to be an end to any threat to Edward's power.[43]

King of the Anglo-Saxons

Alfred the Great had declared himself king of the Anglo-Saxons, and Edward assumed that same title. That was significant in itself. Edward was not only the king of Wessex and Mercia, but he was also the king of all the Anglo-Saxons who were not living in Viking-controlled areas. Many Anglo-Saxons populated the Danelaw, so Edward could conceivably say that he had the right and even the obligation to be the lord and master of those people. His title of King of the Anglo-Saxons could justify his attacks on the Danelaw, as he could say he had the

---

[43] Anglo-Saxons.net. (2023, August 26). *Edward the Elder*. Retrieved from Early-Medieval-England: http://www.anglo-saxons.net/hwaet/?do=get&type=person&id=EdwardtheElder.

intention of annexing territories where the Anglo-Saxons were concentrated.

Lady of the Mercians

Edward had a sister named Æthelflæd. She was a valuable ally of the Wessex king.

To understand her political relationship with Edward, we have to look back at the reign of Alfred the Great. Mercia had been partitioned between the Anglo-Saxons and the Danes after the Battle of Edington, with the former controlling the western portion of Mercia. That part of Mercia came under the control of Æthelred, Lord of the Mercians. He recognized Alfred as his suzerain.

An alliance between Æthelred and Alfred was formalized with the marriage of Æthelred to Alfred's oldest daughter, Æthelflæd. Æthelred was a valuable ally to Alfred and helped repel Viking attacks in the 890s. When Æthelred died in 911, Æthelflæd took her dead husband's place and ruled over the Mercian territory.

An illustration of Æthelflæd.
https://commons.wikimedia.org/wiki/File:%C3%86thelfl%C3%A6d_as_depicted_in_the_cartulary_of_Abingdon_Abbey.png

She continued Æthelred's policy of closely allying with Wessex. That relationship would prove to be pivotal when Edward began to make expansionary movements into the Danelaw.

Æthelflæd was a phenomenon in an age where burly men ruled practically everything. She was a very effective ruler in her own right. William of Malmesbury, an Anglo-Norman chronicler, was effusive in his praise for this woman. In his opinion, Æthelflæd was "a powerful accession to Edward's party, the delight of his subjects, the dread of his enemies, a woman of enlarged soul."[44]

William of Malmesbury was not the only one who appreciated Æthelflæd influence and authority. Modern historians have compared her to Elizabeth I, and her stature nearly overshadows her brother. Together, Æthelflæd and Edward were a dynamic duo that would give the rulers of the Danelaw nightmares.

Building a Bulwark

We do not know much about Edward's reign from the Battle of Holme until 906. He had a truce with the Danes that year, but it was broken, and Vikings raided along the Severn. It was clear that Edward could not trust his neighbors anymore.

Alfred the Great had created a solid defensive line, and Edward improved on it. Æthelflæd joined him in defensive constructions. She built or improved defenses in Wednesbury, Bridgenorth, Tamworth, Stafford, Warwick, Cherbury, and Runcorn. The two rulers created positions that could bolster the defenses of the south against any Danish counterattack.

Edward remained busy. He sent an army into Northumbria in 909 and seized the bones of Saint Oswald (who was king of Northumbria in the 600s) in Lincolnshire. The Danes in Northumbria retaliated with a raid on Mercia. The Vikings were met by an Anglo-Saxon army at the Battle of Tettenhall, where they were defeated. After Tettenhall, the Northumbrian Danes did not go south of the Humber Estuary again, allowing Edward to concentrate on East Anglia and the Five Boroughs.

What is interesting about what happened in those few years is that Edward was encouraging Anglo-Saxons to purchase land in Danish territory. This was likely a move to solidify his claim to the territory since

---

[44] "Order of Medieval Women." https://www.medievalwomen.org/aeligthelflaeligdnbsplady-of-the-mercians.html

more Anglo-Saxons were living in Danish territory.

Another development was in combat. In the preceding years, it was not customary for Anglo-Saxons to wage aggressive, offensive campaigns. Instead, they relied on Danegeld to keep the Vikings happy and at a distance. Edward used Danegeld on occasion, but he became more aggressive as the years passed. He neutralized the Northumbrian Danes, which was a significant victory all by itself. Viking invasions were not as successful as they used to be.

An illustration of Edward the Elder.
https://commons.wikimedia.org/wiki/File:Edward_the_Elder_-_MS_Royal_14_B_VI.jpg

Æthelflæd went on the offensive as well. An army she sent in 917 to Derby resulted in her taking control of a significant borough of the Danelaw. This is considered her greatest triumph. The year 917 is also the year in which East Anglian Danes submitted to Edward.

Æthelflæd took control of Leicester in 918 and received the submission of the local Danish army. The great lady died in 918, and Mercia was absorbed into Wessex.

Edward continued to build forts in places like Towcester and Maldon. His armies continued to be successful against Danish troops, even taking Nottingham. The *Anglo-Saxon Chronicle* of 918 had this to say about Edward's accomplishments: "And all of the people who had settled in Mercia, both Danish and English, submitted to him."[45]

Edward had effective control of all lands south of the Humber. Northumbria continued to be contested, but Edward accomplished a great deal in a few years. The concept of England as a unified country was increasingly becoming a reality, thanks to the efforts of Edward and Æthelflæd.

Letters and the Arts

Edward was an effective warrior because he had to be one. Holding on to a crown in the Middle Ages was a 24/7 job, and he needed to be on the alert for any possible threats. This did not mean that his reign was only battles and sieges. While Edward was not as academically inclined as his father, he was schooled by the scholars at his father's court and was a knowledgeable man.

We do not know how far he pursued Alfred the Great's programs for education reform, but the written script known as Anglo-Saxon square minuscule, a form of calligraphy used in the Middle Ages that made the Latin alphabet more recognizable, has its early phases in Edward's reign. We do know that there were scholarly centers in Canterbury, Winchester, and Worcester.

The surviving large-scale embroideries made in Anglo-Saxon England go back to Edward's reign. These items were taken from the coffin of Saint Cuthbert, and they were commissioned by Edward's second wife.

Edward was also responsible for the construction of the New Minster in Winchester. It was a royal abbey Edward commissioned because he wanted a building that was much grander than the older one.

A Mighty King

Edward's success in bringing England under his control is exemplified by a passage in the *Anglo-Saxon Chronicle*:

"Then Edward went from there into the Peak District to Bakewell and ordered a borough to be built in the neighborhood and manned. And then the king of the Scots and all the people of the Scots, and Raegnald and the sons of Eadwulf and all who live in Northumbria, both

---

[45] "Edward the Elder." http://www.anglo-saxons.net/hwaet/?do=get&type=person&id=EdwardtheElder.

English and Danish, Norsemen and others, and also the king of the Strathclyde Welsh and all the Strathclyde Welsh chose him as father and Lord."[46]

There has been some dispute over whether this portion of the *Anglo-Saxon Chronicle* is accurate, but there's little doubt that after twenty years of campaigns, Edward had absolute control of the land south of the Humber and had the Danes on the back foot.

King Edward the Elder died in 924 while on a campaign against the Welsh. His successor, Æthelstan, was as competent a king as his father and grandfather.

Æthelstan

Æthelstan was the son of Edward the Elder and the king's consort, Ecgwynn. Æthelstan would be a credit to his father and is considered one of the greatest kings of England.

Æthelstan carried on a tradition begun by Alfred the Great: serving as a competent king of Wessex. The reputation of this monarchy was impressive, and modern-day medieval historian Veronica Ortenberg elaborated on their status, which they even enjoyed overseas.

"Wessex kings carried an aura of power and success, which made them increasingly powerful in the 920s while most Continental houses were in military trouble and engaged in internecine warfare period. While the civil wars and Viking attacks on the Continent had spelled the end of unity of the Carolingian empire, which had already disintegrated into separate kingdoms, military success had enabled Æthelstan to triumph at home and attempt to go beyond the reputation of a great heroic dynasty of warrior kings, in order to develop a Carolingian ideology of kingship."

She goes further to claim that Æthelstan was thought of as the new Charlemagne by European rulers. The days of weak Anglo-Saxon kings were long gone.[47]

---

[46] Davidson, Michael R. (2001). "The (Non)submission of the Northern Kings in 920". In Higham, N. J.; Hill, D. H. (eds.). Edward the Elder, 899–924. Abingdon, UK: Routledge. pp. 200–211. ISBN 978-0-415-21497-1.

[47] Ortenberg, Veronica (2010). "The King from Overseas: Why did Æthelstan Matter in Tenth-Century Continental Affairs?" In Rollason, David; Leyser, Conrad; Williams, Hannah (eds.). England and the Continent in the Tenth Century: Studies in Honour of Wilhelm Levison (1876–1947). Turnhout, Belgium: Brepols.

A 15th-century stained-glass window of Æthelstan.
https://commons.wikimedia.org/wiki/File:Athelstan_from_All_Souls_College_Chapel.jpg

Æthelstan's succession was contested. His half-brother, Aelfweard, laid claim to the throne, and a civil war could have occurred. Fortunately for Æthelstan, Aelfweard died a few weeks after the death of Edward the Elder. Thus, a bloody war was avoided.

Æthelstan did not take any chances as far as his crown was concerned. He banished his brother Edwin to avoid any more controversy. (Some historians believe he fled to avoid his brother's wrath.) Edwin died in a shipwreck. Æthelstan regretted having to force his brother out of the kingdom. However, it needs to be remembered that these were tough times. The Vikings in the Danelaw were still there to the north and threatened Wessex's stability. Æthelstan had an obligation not just to himself but also to his subjects to see to it that the kingdom had stable leadership. He was going to make good on his responsibilities.[48]

All or Nothing

A cache of coins from the 10th century was found near Harrogate. One coin, in particular, bore an interesting inscription: "Rex totius Britanniæ" ("King of all Britain"). It was from the time that Æthelstan was the king of Wessex, and it best describes his ultimate goal. Æthelstan wanted not to be just the king of the Anglo-Saxons. Æthelstan wished to rule all of England, and he was going to try to do so.

A devout Christian, Æthelstan was probably tired of the laissez-faire attitude that the Vikings in the Danelaw had toward religious conversion. In 926, he gave one of his sisters to Sitric of Northumbria on the condition that Sitric would convert to Christianity. Sitric agreed, but soon after the marriage, he went back to worshiping the old Norse gods. Sitric died the following year, and his cousin, Guthfrith of Ivar, tried to succeed him. That was not acceptable to Æthelstan, so he drove the other man out.[49]

The Anglo-Saxon king went further. Æthelstan captured York. The significance of that conquest cannot be overstated. It was the first time that a king of Wessex gained control of a piece of northern territory. He received the submission of the Danish people of York, which infuriated other Northumbrians, as they did not want to be controlled by a southern power.

Their outrage did not matter. On July 12th, 927, at Eamont, King Constantine II of Alba (Scotland), King Hywel Dda of Deheubarth

---

[48] Ross, D. (2023, August 26). *King Æthelstan*. Retrieved from Britainexpress.com: https://www.britainexpress.com/History/Æthelstan.htm.

[49] Erenow.net. (2023, August 26). *The Danelaw II*. Retrieved from Erenow.net: https://erenow.net/postclassical/thevikingsahistory/12.php.

(Wales), Ealdred of Bamburgh, and King Owain of Strathclyde (a Scottish kingdom near the River Clyde) accepted Æthelstan as their overlord. The idea of a man being king of Britain was coming closer to being a reality.

A map of Britain and Ireland in the 10th century.
Ikonact, CC BY-SA 3.0 <https://creativecommons.org/licenses/by-sa/3.0>, via Wikimedia Commons; https://commons.wikimedia.org/wiki/File:British_Isles_10th_century.svg

Æthelstan the Lawgiver

The time of peace gave Æthelstan a chance to turn his attention to other matters. The king was particularly interested in law. The Anglo-Saxons had a long history of using legal codes, and the statutes were written in the vernacular. Æthelstan took up where Alfred the Great left off. We have a massive number of legal texts that survived from his reign.

Clerical matters were essential to Æthelstan. His tithe edict is thought to be the earliest surviving law from his reign. Æthelstan introduced codes that emphasized the importance of paying tithes to the church. He was concerned about the poor, so his law code stated the amount of money that should be given to people experiencing poverty.

Threats to the social order, particularly robbery, drew his attention. The law code that he issued at Grateley mandated harsh penalties, which included the death penalty for a person over twelve years old who was caught in the act of stealing goods worth more than eight pence. Æthelstan would later raise the minimum age of the death penalty to fifteen because he believed it was not right to kill people who were so young.

Some modern historians view Æthelstan's legislation as being too harsh, but it must be remembered that the king was dealing with a rough population. Æthelstan was committed to maintaining a social code of order, and he was strict with officials, demanding their respect for the law and expecting them to do their duties diligently.

Administration

Æthelstan worked to institute a centralized government. Charters produced during his reign show his commitment to royal control over important activities.

Æthelstan made use of councils comprised of important people to exert royal authority outside of Wessex. These assemblies served to break down obstacles to the unification of England. Historian John Maddicott believed these gatherings were the beginning of formal assemblies that proved to be "the true if unwitting founder of the English parliament."[50]

---

[50] Maddicott, John (2010). The Origins of the English Parliament, 924-1327. Oxford, UK: Oxford University Press.

Relations with the Church

Æthelstan founded churches and gave generously to monasteries. He maintained a close relationship with the church hierarchy and appointed bishops. Those he selected were often close to him. Ælfheah and Beornstan, priests who said Mass for his household, were made bishops of Wells and Winchester, respectively.

Æthelstan liked to collect relics and was known to have an extensive collection. He donated relics and manuscripts to monasteries and was a devotee of the cult of Saint Cuthbert.

Learning

Æthelstan mimicked his grandfather in his commitment to learning and ecclesiastical scholarship. His reputation for promoting education drew scholars to his court. The court was a scholarly hub for the revival of the hermeneutic style of Latin writing. An unknown scribe whom historians have dubbed "Æthelstan A" was responsible for drafting charters. His style of writing is considered the best writing of the Anglo-Saxon tradition.

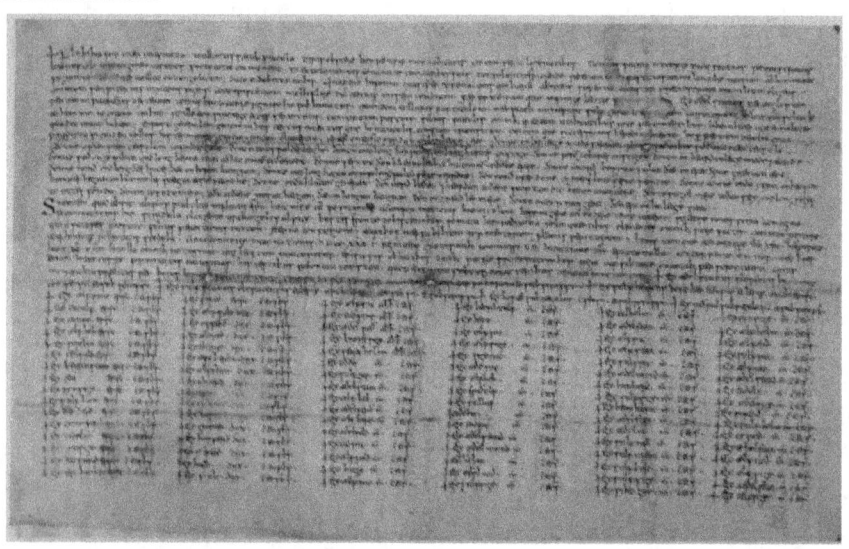

An example of the "Æthelstan A" charters.
https://commons.wikimedia.org/wiki/File:Charter_S416_written_by_%C3%86thelstan_A_in_931.jpg

Troubles in Scotland

Æthelstan had made himself the most powerful ruler in England since the Roman times, but his authority was subject to challenges. Scotland renounced its allegiance in 933, and Æthelstan had to respond.

He assembled a large army at Winchester in 934 and headed north to Scotland. It was a military force that had not been seen before. Æthelstan had a mounted army and a naval force that went up the English coast and into Scottish waters up to Caithness.[51]

Æthelstan was able to reestablish himself, but trouble was still brewing. The Scots were not finished annoying the king.

King Constantine of Scotland forged an alliance with Olaf of Dublin, whom Æthelstan had earlier driven from York, and King Owen of Strathclyde in 937. Olaf raided Mercia, causing Æthelstan to march north with his brother, Edmund.[52]

The Battle of Brunanburh

The Battle of Brunanburh is referred to as the greatest single battle in Anglo-Saxon history before the Battle of Hastings. The site of the engagement is unknown, but the Wirral Peninsula has been suggested as the battleground. What we know about the contest is that the Celtic/Norse alliance was entrenched on the field, and Æthelstan's army mounted a cavalry charge directly at them. The *Annals of Ulster* give a description of what happened:

"A huge war, lamentable and horrible, was cruelly waged between the Saxons and the Norsemen. Many thousands of Norsemen beyond number died although King Anlaf [Olaf Guthfrithson] escaped with a few men. While a great number of the Saxons also fell on the other side, Æthelstan, king of the Saxons, was enriched by the great victor."[53]

The *Anglo-Saxon Chronicle* also recorded the battle in a long poem that includes these lines:

"Five kings lay on the field of battle, in bloom of youth, pierce with swords. So seven eke of the earls of Anlaf; and of the ship's crew unnumber'd crowds."[54]

The casualties were probably exaggerated. The outcome solidified the northern borders of England and kept the Celts in the west. The

---

[51] Garner, T. (2018, January 2). *Michael Wood on Æthelstan's "Great War" to Unite Anglo-Saxon England.* Retrieved from Historyanswers.co.uk: https://www.historyanswers.co.uk/history-of-war/michael-wood-on-Æthelstans-great-war-to-unite-anglo-saxon-england/.

[52] Erenow.net. *The Danelaw II.*

[53] English Monarchs. (2023, August 23). *The Battle of Brunanburh.* Retrieved from Englishmonarchs.co.uk: https://www.englishmonarchs.co.uk/brunanburh.html.

[54] English Monarchs. *The Battle of Brunanburh.*

significance of the Battle of Brunanburh is that it established, without a doubt, a unified kingdom of England. Æthelstan had full control of Wessex and Mercia.

Æthelstan died in 939 and was succeeded by his brother Edmund, who inherited the title "King of the English." Æthelstan only ruled for less than a decade, but his accomplishments were impressive. Many historians consider Æthelstan to be the father of medieval and modern England. There are those who object to this, but nearly everyone admits that Æthelstan compares favorably to Alfred the Great.

Æthelstan's reputation reached beyond the borders of his kingdom. He was held in high regard in Europe and established good connections on the Continent. Æthelstan completed the work started by his grandfather and father. His legacy as a capable warrior, administrator, and advocate for learning are well deserved.

However, the story of Anglo-Saxon England and the Vikings is not finished. Small raids were becoming rare, but it did not mean the island was safe and sound. Anglo-Saxon England was going to face a substantial threat from the northwest. Political developments in Scandinavia would eventually lead to an empire that was nearly the size of what Charlemagne ruled.

Chapter Seven: Sweyn Forkbeard and Cnut the Great

Forward to Catastrophe

Æthelstan left a strong kingdom to his successor, Edmund. The royal work of over fifty years seemed almost complete. England was a country with a strong administration, a legal code that was somewhat fair (at least for the period), and an economy that was doing great. Everything seemed to be going well for Anglo-Saxon England. However, there was a rule to be followed. Whoever was king could be one as long as he was able to protect the crown. And that was not always a guarantee.

Edmund was a young man when he assumed the throne. The former king was barely cold in his coffin when Olaf of Dublin was accepted as the king of York. He capitalized on his new title by reclaiming the Five Boroughs that had been initially taken by Edward the Elder. Olaf died a few years later, and Edmund was able to regain what had been lost.

However, his success did not guarantee that everything was going to be quiet. The king was required to put down a rebellion in Wales and was also required to deal with a troublesome situation in Scotland.

Still, Edmund was able to maintain overlordship until disaster struck. Edmund was killed in a brawl and left sons who were too young to rule. His successor was Eadred, his younger brother.

Eadred was required to deal with problems that sprang up in Northumbria. The situation was fluid, to say the least. Northumbrian magnates accepted Eadred as king but reneged on that promise and swore loyalty instead to Eric Bloodaxe. Eadred responded with a vicious raid on Northumbria. Even though he lost a battle at Castleford, Eadred was able to coerce the Northumbrians into renouncing Eric. Eadred died in 955 and was succeeded by Eadwig, the eldest son of Edmund, who died in 959.

It is important to note that the Anglo-Saxons had three kings in the span of twenty-two years. Before that, the people had three kings in sixty-eight years. The three later kings were almost constantly at war, trying to hold on to their possessions and putting down revolts. There was very little time for the stability required to nurture a peaceful society. The Anglo-Saxon kingdom that Æthelstan bequeathed to his heirs became a fairly unstable kingdom within twenty years after his death.

End of the Danelaw

Eadred did not live long enough to make a lasting impact on Anglo-Saxon history, but one very important development happened during his time on the throne. Eric Bloodaxe was driven out of York, and the people of Northumbria pledged their allegiance to the Anglo-Saxon king. The Danelaw was no more.

The Anglo-Saxons could hardly be blamed if they expressed good riddance to this northern neighbor. The Danelaw was a Viking outpost in England and a potential source of trouble. Treaties with the Anglo-Saxons were broken, and no one trusted the Norsemen on the border. The final collapse of the Danelaw would permit the Anglo-Saxon kings to have better control over the land. Surely, there would be less trouble. Or so everyone thought.

The kingdom was divided in 957, with Edgar, son of Edmund, ruling Mercia and Eadwig having suzerainty over Wessex. Edgar assumed the crown over all of England when Eadwig died in 959.

Edgar's reign differed from earlier administrations because there were no Viking raids while he ruled. His reign was viewed as a peaceful time without external threats or internal trouble. That was not to last, though.

His successor, Edward the Martyr, was murdered in 978. The man who took the next, Æthelred the Unready, would go down in history as a monarch who faced extraordinary challenges that had not been seen in Anglo-Saxon England for years.

Æthelred's reign endured raids from the Danish Vikings. These raids began in the 980s and became gradually worse. Attacks occurred all along the coastline. The brunt of the assaults was felt by the counties of

Cheshire, Thanet, Hampshire, Cornwell, Devon, and Dorset. The problems with the raids were made worse by the lords of Normandy, who permitted the marauding Danes to take refuge in their territory. Papal intervention facilitated a peace treaty in 991, but that did not stop the violence.[55]

Battle of Maldon

The Battle of Maldon would be memorialized in an Old English poem titled "The Battle of Maldon." This conflict was a disaster for the Anglo-Saxons. An army of Norwegian Vikings was confronted by East Saxons led by Ealdorman Byrhtnoth on the River Blackwater in Essex in 991. The Vikings were led by Olaf Tryggvason, who would later become king of Norway.

The Vikings were stationed on an island called Northey. There was a causeway that led to the island. The battle began when high tide covered the causeway. When the water receded, the Vikings asked to be let across to fight on the mainland. The Anglo-Saxons allowed them to do so and were defeated after their commander was killed. We will let the reader decide if the Anglo-Saxons were being polite or foolish for permitting the Vikings to cross over.[56]

The Return of Danegeld Payments

Historians note that Æthelred was often the victim of incredibly bad advice. After the defeat at Maldon, the king was advised to pay tribute to the Vikings in the hope that they would be satisfied with the cash and go away. The amount of the tribute is estimated to have been £10,000.

It appears that no one bothered to look at the history books to determine if the Vikings would actually respect those arrangements. The Vikings did not follow the terms of the agreement, and attacks continued along the coastline. London was assaulted by a large Viking fleet in 994. That fleet was a combined effort led by Olaf Tryggvason, the victor of Maldon, and Danish King Sweyn Forkbeard.

Scandinavian Nation-states

The land of the Vikings changed. It was no longer a place where clans fought blood feuds and disputes were settled with trial by combat. The

---

[55] Brain, J. (2023, August 27). *King Æthelred The Unready*. Retrieved from Historic-uk.com: https://www.historic-uk.com/HistoryUK/HistoryofEngland/Æthelred-The-Unready/.

[56] E. H. Seigfried, K. (2015, November 6). *The Battle of Maldon*. Retrieved from The Norse Mythology Blog: https://www.norsemyth.org/2015/11/the-battle-of-maldon.html.

north was becoming "civilized."

Sweyn Forkbeard was the product of the nation-state of Denmark. He was the son of Danish King Harald Bluetooth, who is credited with the conversion of Denmark to Christianity. Sweyn was not a devout Christian, but he accepted it for political reasons while tolerating the old pagan beliefs.

Sweyn was an ambitious man who made his own luck. He led a successful rebellion against his father; Harald died during the revolt. Sweyn raided London with Olaf Tryggvason but turned against his former ally a few years later and helped defeat Olaf at the Battle of Svolder in 1000. The victory allowed Sweyn to gain a portion of Norway as direct ruler and other parts of the country as a feudal overlord.[57]

Medieval Ethnic Cleansing

The raids on England continued. Hampshire, Sussex, and Dorset were pillaged in 997. Æthelred secured another truce with the Vikings for a payment of £24,000 in 1001, but this was no doubt a temporary arrangement. The king was aware the Vikings would return.

Æthelred the Unready needed to watch his back. A fifth column might have existed in the territories of the former Danelaw, whose inhabitants likely were more loyal to their blood ties than to the crown. The king received intelligence that suggested the Danes were plotting to kill him and his advisors. So, Æthelred decided to strike first. On November 13th, 1002, the king ordered the massacre of all Danish men living in the realm.

There is no record of precisely how many people were murdered. One story recorded in a charter of 1004 tells of Danish families in Oxford breaking into a church for sanctuary and the local people burning down the church and roasting the Danes inside.

Æthelred justified his actions by claiming that the decree had been issued on the advice of his leading men. If so, it was a piece of advice that had terrifying consequences.

Gunnhild, the sister of Sweyn Forkbeard, was one of the dead in Oxford. Sweyn was enraged by the news and sacked Exeter in retaliation.

---

[57] English History. (2023, August 27). *Sweyn Forkbeard*. Retrieved from Englishhistory.net: https://englishhistory.net/vikings/sweyn-forkbeard/.

He went on to harass Wessex and destroy Wilton.[58]

King of England

The Viking raids intensified. Sweyn probably was no longer trying to avenge his sister's death but instead was looking for permanent control of England. He invaded England in 1013 and ultimately forced Æthelred to flee for his life. Sweyn was declared king of England but died a few weeks later, on February 3rd, 1014.

Æthelred returned from exile and drove Sweyn's followers out, but he was then forced to deal with a significant Viking invasion. Embattled and with little military support, Æthelred died on April 23rd, 1016. He lived to see Cnut, Sweyn's son, arrive in England with a massive force, but he did not live to see what Cnut accomplished.[59]

Æthelred the Unready's historical reputation has been slightly rehabilitated in recent years. In retrospect, it seems the king was a victim of circumstances that were not easy to manage, and he received some very poor advice from his counselors. His reign was the longest of all the Anglo-Saxon kings, and there were some accomplishments. Unfortunately, those are often overshadowed by his constant problems with the Danish Vikings.

---

[58] Cavendish, R. (2002, November). *The St. Brice's Day Massacre.* Retrieved from History Today: https://www.historytoday.com/archive/st-brice%E2%80%99s-day-massacre.

[59] Brain, J. *King Æthelred The Unready.*

An illustration of Æthelred the Unready.
https://commons.wikimedia.org/wiki/File:Ethelred_the_Unready.jpg

Æthelred was succeeded by his son Edmund Ironside (also known as Edmund II), who ruled briefly. When Edmund died, the new king was someone who is considered one of the most powerful monarchs of the Middle Ages.

Cnut (Canute) the Great

Cnut was the son of Sweyn Forkbeard and was born around 990, although the exact date is unknown. Cnut would become one of the most significant rulers of the Middle Ages, as he was the king of England, Denmark, and Norway. His united realm would be known as the North Sea Empire.

Cnut was the last prominent Viking king. The age of seafaring raiders was coming to an end and would soon be replaced by nation-states with foreign policies that did not include other areas for the sake of gaining loot. Cnut was a Christian who used his religion to further his own purposes.

A drawing of King Cnut.
https://commons.wikimedia.org/wiki/File:Canute_and_%C3%86lfgifu_cropped_(Canute).jpg

He accompanied his father in 1013 when Sweyn invaded England for the last time. Sweyn's domain was divided at his death in 1014, and his other son, Harald II, became the king of Denmark. Olaf II was crowned king of Norway.

Cnut was not automatically made king of England; the English chose to restore Æthelred to the throne. That did not sit well with Cnut, who had counted on the oaths of allegiance given by Anglo-Saxon nobles. His army was too small to fight Æthelred, so Cnut sailed back to Denmark. However, before he left English waters, Cnut slaughtered the hostages who had been given to his father as pledges of loyalty. The young man was making it clear to the Anglo-Saxons that he was angry and would seek his revenge later.

Harald II was not comfortable with having Cnut in Denmark. To get his younger brother out of the way, Harald offered to support an invasion of England on the condition that Cnut would renounce any claim to the Danish throne. Cnut knew England was a bigger prize than Denmark, so he agreed to Harald's offer.

A Savage Arrival

Cnut raised an army of ten thousand men, and his strike force landed in Wessex, which he was able to subdue without much difficulty. He was supported in his invasion by Eadric Streona, the ealdorman of Mercia, who deserted Æthelred.

Cnut was out for revenge against those who had betrayed him. He moved north to Northumbria, overwhelmed it, and executed the ealdorman, Uhtred. Uhtred's death was his punishment for breaking his loyalty oath to Sweyn.

Cnut continued his war of conquest by besieging London in 1016. He soon began to deal with Æthelred's successor, Edmund Ironside. After winning the Battle of Assandun in October 1016, Cnut negotiated with Edmund.

The result was a division of England that gave Wessex to Edmund and the rest of England to Cnut. Edmund died the following January, which made Cnut the ruler of all England. Cnut celebrated his succession by executing nobles who had violated their oath of allegiance to his father and seizing the estates of other miscreants. Those lands were divided among his soldiers and other loyal followers. Cnut wanted to kill Edmund Ironside's small children, but they were able to flee and gain asylum in Hungary.[60]

---

[60] Mingren, W. (2020, May 21). *Cnut the Great: The Myth, the Man, and the Multi-National Viking Monarch*. Retrieved from Ancient Origins: https://www.ancient-origins.net/history-

The English King

Cnut's reign of terror was over, and he got down to the business of being a monarch. He divided England into four earldoms.: Northumbria, Mercia, Wessex, and East Anglia. He married Emma, Æthelred the Unready's widow, in 1017, thereby neutralizing any challenge to his kingship that could come from the surviving children of Æthelred.[61]

Cnut did not want any more trouble in England. He recalled the Viking fleet of thirty ships in 1018 and decided to settle with the army that had followed him from Denmark. The settlement was straightforward: Cnut paid them off using the tax system that was already in place. The new king also raised £82,500 to pay the army and sent them back to Denmark. Cnut reduced his naval fleet to forty ships to bring peace and stability to the realm.

Cnut convened a council of Anglo-Saxons and Danes. An agreement was reached by which everyone was to live in peace, and Cnut would govern based on the laws and traditions that were in place before his accession.[62]

All of these actions showed that Cnut was more than a marauding pirate. He used statecraft instead of a warpath to consolidate his control over his kingdom. England was a peaceful kingdom during his reign. That was important because Cnut had a new opportunity to pursue.

Harald II died in 1018, and Cnut returned to Denmark to claim the vacant throne. He left behind a letter to the English nation, warning everyone to behave themselves in no uncertain terms:

"If anyone, ecclesiastic or layman, Dane, or Englishman, is so presumptuous as to defy God's law and my royal authority or the secular laws, and he will not make amends and desist according to the direction of my bishops, I do pray, and also command, Earl Thurkil, if he can, to cause the evil-dealer to do right. And if he cannot, then it is my will that with the power of us both he shall destroy him in the land, or drive him

---

famous-people/cnut-great-0013741.

[61] Parker, E. (2016, October). *Cnut: The Great Dane*. Retrieved from History Extra: https://www.historyextra.com/period/anglo-saxon/king-cnut-danish-why-called-great-rule-england-success/.

[62] Abernethy, S. (2014, January 24). *Cnut England's Danish King*. Retrieved from The Freelance History Writer: https://thefreelancehistorywriter.com/2014/01/24/cnut-englands-danish-king/.

out of the land, whether he be of high or low rank. And it is my will that all the nation, ecclesiastical and lay, shall steadfastly observe Edgar's laws, which all men have chosen and sworn at Oxford."[63]

Cnut was speaking with the authority of a man who expected to be obeyed by his subjects. His previous behavior gave a good indication of what he would do if anybody tried to cross him.

Internal Politics

Cnut could be reasonably adept at royal politics. Instead of surrounding himself with Danes, he allowed Anglo-Saxons to hold important positions, such as the earldoms of Wessex and Mercia. Cnut was quick to dismiss people who were not up to his expectations. Thorkell the Tall, whom Cnut initially placed in charge of East Anglia, was outlawed in 1021.

Cnut recognized the importance of the Christian Church. He made all the outward appearances of being devout, but it must be remembered that he was a pragmatic ruler. He knew that the approval of the church would go a long way. He maintained good relations with the church hierarchy. Royal gifts to the church, including tax exemptions and grants of land, were generous. Cnut gave large gifts of money to the church, and he was a benefactor of monasteries. His actions suggest that he was able to bind the church close to him so he would not have to worry about trouble coming from the bishops.

Trip to Rome

Cnut traveled to Rome in 1027 to attend the coronation of Conrad II as the Holy Roman emperor. This allowed him to get to know Conrad and demonstrate to others that he was a pious Christian and a devoted follower of the Christian Church.

Cnut made a great impression from all accounts. He had a chance to do some favors for his subjects while he was in Rome. English pilgrims were given a reduced toll tax and were safeguarded on their way to Rome.

Trouble in Scandinavia

While things were relatively quiet in England, there were some difficulties in Scandinavia that Cnut needed to sort out. He left Denmark and placed a caretaker, Ulf Jarl, in charge. Ulf Jarl was made the earl of

---

[63] Trow, M. J. (2005), *Cnut – Emperor of the North*, Stroud: Sutton.

Denmark (Ulf was also Cnut's brother-in-law).

Trouble with Sweden and Norway caused Cnut to go back to Scandinavia. He defeated the Swedes and Norwegians at the Battle of Helgeå in 1025. Cnut also had a family matter to resolve. It is believed that Ulf Jarl betrayed Cnut. Although Ulf eventually returned to support Cnut, the king did not fully forgive the betrayal. He eventually ordered Ulf's murder. Ulf Jarl was killed in a church.

Cnut moved against Norway. Olaf II had taken the throne in 1016, and Cnut wanted it back. In 1028, Cnut succeeded in driving Olaf II from his throne. Olaf's attempt to regain his throne failed. Cnut was now the king of Norway, England, and Denmark.

Master of All He Surveyed

Cnut had authority over England, Denmark, Norway, parts of Sweden, and some areas in Scotland and Ireland. He was a patron of Old Norse poetry, and his wife Emma was a patron of literature. His court was multi-national, and he had a reputation as being a wise and skillful monarch.

Cnut was also the subject of a popular legend that was recorded years later in the Historia Anglorum (*History of the English*). Cnut had to listen to a lot of flattery from the court, and he wanted to prove how empty their words were. He did so in a unique way.

Tired of being told how high and mighty he was, Cnut ordered a chair be placed on the seashore while the tide was coming in. He sat on the chair, pronounced he was overlord of the sea, and commanded the waves to stop rolling onto his land. Naturally, the waves disobeyed and kept coming in, drenching the king's legs. Cnut jumped back and declared that the power of earthly kings was empty and only God could command the waves. There are several versions of this story, but the tale shows that Cnut was smart enough to know his limitations and reminded his courtiers that their pretty words did not easily move him.

Cnut died on November 12th, 1035, in Shaftesbury. His empire quickly fell apart. Harold I (Harold Harefoot) succeeded him in England. Harthacnut took the throne in 1040, and in 1042, Edward the Confessor was crowned king.

Cnut's coronation showed the ultimate integration of Danes and Anglo-Saxons in England. The nation was no longer divided between one group and another; instead, it was a unified country. It had a tradition of law, culture, and literature, which made England stand out from the rest of Europe.

There is still one more chapter to be written about the Vikings and the Anglo-Saxons. This time, the descendants of the original sea raiders took center stage.

Chapter Eight: Stamford Bridge and Hastings

Anglo-Saxon England had a peculiar habit of canonizing barely competent monarchs. Edmund the Martyr, Edward the Martyr, and Edward the Confessor were known for leading very pious lives but having little clue about how to manage royal politics. They were holy saints at a time when Anglo-Saxon England needed pragmatic sinners. The common people would suffer from the lack of stable leadership.

Edward the Confessor was the son of Æthelred the Unready. He was born at a time when the Danes were taking the upper hand in England, and Æthelred was barely able to hold on to power. Edward was forced to flee with his mother, Emma, to Normandy after Sweyn Forkbeard took the throne. Edward spent most of his boyhood living in exile in Normandy. He had the support of many people who felt that Edward had a legitimate claim to the throne. One of his supporters was Robert I, Duke of Normandy, who went as far as to attempt an invasion to put Edward on the throne.[64]

Bloody Family Politics

When Sweyn died, Æthelred was invited to come back to rule. Edward came along with him. Æthelred died in 1016, and his son, Edmund Ironside, took over. He died later that year, and Cnut took

---

[64] Brain, J. (2023, August 29). *Edward the Confessor*. Retrieved from Historic-uk.com: https://www.historic-uk.com/HistoryUK/HistoryofEngland/Edward-The-Confessor/.

power. Edward went into exile with his siblings, but things soon became strange.

Cnut convinced Emma, Æthelred's widow, to marry him. The marriage produced Harthacnut, who became king of Denmark on Cnut's death. Harold Harefoot, the half-brother of Harthacnut, became king of England (Cnut had killed Edward's last surviving older half-brother, Eadwig). Harthacnut gathered a fleet to invade England in 1039. Emma supported Harthacnut for the throne over Edward despite Edward being her son with Æthelred the Unready. However, Harold died before the invasion could begin. Harthacnut succeeded Harold Harefoot as king of England in 1040.

This succession merry-go-round is enough to make a person dizzy. The important point is that Harthacnut was the son of Cnut, while Edward was the child of the last Anglo-Saxon king of Wessex. Harthacnut invited Edward back to England in 1041, and Edward was viewed as the eventual successor. Harthacnut died on June 8th, 1042.

The English people favored Edward to become the next monarch. In the words of the *Anglo-Saxon Chronicle*, "Before he [Harthacnut] was buried, all the people chose Edward as king in London."[65] Edward got even with his mother for her lack of support the following year. He formally stripped her of her property, and she faded from history, eventually dying in 1052.

The controversies that began with Cnut's death and ended with Edward's coronation underscore the discord and confusion that surrounded the English crown in those years. Half-brothers would take the throne and kill other half-brothers in order to keep it. There apparently was no loyalty within the royal family, and one relative would treat the other as a grave enemy. One example is what happened to Alfred, Edward's brother. He was brutally murdered by Harold Harefoot despite being a stepbrother to the king.

Godwin of Wessex

The power behind the throne for almost half of Edward the Confessor's reign was Godwin of Wessex. He played a principal role in the Machiavellian politics of 11th-century England. Cnut made Godwin the earl of Wessex in 1018. Godwin was responsible for the death of Edward's brother, Alfred, because he turned Alfred over to Harold

---

[65] Giles, J.A. (1914). *The Anglo-Saxon Chronicle*. London: G. Bell and Sonson. p. 114.

Harefoot.

What kept Godwin alive was the immense power he possessed. Wessex was a dominant earldom, and Godwin was a wealthy man. The earl's true allegiance was to himself, and though he was initially a supporter of Harthacnut, he deftly switched sides to ally with Edward the Confessor. That relationship became more robust in 1045 when Godwin's daughter, Edith, was married to King Edward.[66]

Edward chaffed under Godwin's dominance, and the tensions came to a head in 1051. Edward appointed a Norman named Robert of Jumièges as the archbishop of Canterbury. A clash in Dover prompted Edward to order Godwin, who was also the earl of Kent, to punish the town, but Godwin refused. Godwin's two sons, Sweyn and Harold, raised an army from their vassals and threatened Gloucester, where Edward was holding court. Edward's allies raised another army to counter that force. A crisis was averted when it was agreed that the meeting of the royal council, the Witan, would later convene in London.

Edward decided to press his advantage and called on all the militias of England. Godwin's own men were obliged to be part of that levy, and his sons fled to Flanders and Ireland. Edward went further in severing connections with the Godwin family by sending Edith to a nunnery.

Godwin returned in 1052 with an army. Edward was forced to restore Godwin and his sons to their estates, and Edith was restored as queen. Everything seemed to be working well for Godwin when something unexpected happened.

At a royal banquet in Winchester, Godwin denied he had anything to do with the death of Alfred, which had occurred years before. The *Anglo-Saxon Chronicle* recounts the story:

"On Easter Monday, as he was sitting with the king at a meal, he suddenly sank toward the footstool, bereft of speech, and deprived of all his strength. Then he was carried to the king's private room and they thought it was about to pass off. But it was not so. On the contrary, he continued like this without speech or strength right on to the Thursday and then departed this life."[67]

---

[66] Zimmerman, M. (2023, August 29). *Earl Godwin, The Lesser Known Kingmaker*. Retrieved from Historic-uk.com: https://www.historic-uk.com/HistoryUK/HistoryofEngland/Earl-Godwin/.

[67] Douglas, David C. (1990) William the Conqueror: The Norman Impact Upon England London: Methuen. Pg. 412.

Godwin was dead. His family was still a powerful force in England, but it did not have control over Edward the Confessor. However, Godwin's successor as earl of Wessex, Harold Godwinson, was an influential lord, and his brothers had positions of authority in England at the time of Edward the Confessor's death.

The Norman Connection

Some of the problems that Edward the Confessor had with the earl of Wessex stemmed from the growing influence of the Normans in Edward's court. Edward lived under the protection of the dukes of Normandy for years, and the English king had not forgotten this kindness. Robert of Jumièges, who was from Normandy, was an advisor to the king before he was appointed to the Archbishopric of Canterbury. Edward appointed Normans to be sheriffs in England.

We do not have a clear picture of exactly how much influence the Normans had in Edward's court. However, there is no doubt the presence of Normans was sufficient enough to make Godwin and his sons leery. The concern was well founded because the Normans would soon play a significant role in the royal succession.

The Final Years

Edward's reign after Godwin's death included vigorous campaigns against the Scots and the Welsh. However, he appeared to withdraw from active politics to go hunting. His reputation as a religiously devoted man includes the completion of Westminster Abbey, a jewel in his crown.

Even though Edward had deep religious convictions, he was still a king and had to protect his throne. He did harsh things, such as ordering the assassination of a Welsh prince. Edward's many years in exile deprived him of the ability to create a power base, so he was at odds with the earls in his realm.

A significant problem was his succession. Edward did not have any children, and he gave no clear indication of who would be his successor, which was a considerable mistake. In the opinion of historian Stephen David Baxter, Edward's "handling of the succession issue was dangerously indecisive, and continued to be one of the greatest catastrophes to which the English have ever succumbed."[68]

---

[68] Baxter, Stephen (2009). "Edward the Confessor and the Succession Question". In Mortimer, Richard (ed.). Edward the Confessor: The Man and the Legend. Woodbridge: Boydell Press.

January 5th, 1066, was the beginning of the end of Anglo-Saxon England. Edward the Confessor died that day and set in motion the events that would end with a decisive battle waged on the English southern shore. On the following day, January 6th, the Witan proclaimed Harold Godwinson to be the new king of England. He was the late king's brother-in-law. He was a very competent and powerful earl, which was sufficient enough for the Witan to make him king.

The Viking Claimant

There was a claimant to the throne in Scandinavia. The Norwegian Harald Hardrada is celebrated as the last great Viking. He was the youngest brother of King Olaf II of Norway, and he was a committed warrior.

He fought with his brother at the Battle of Stiklestad in 1030 against Cnut. Olaf was killed in the fight, and Harald barely escaped. Afterward, he became a professional mercenary and served with distinction in the Byzantine Empire and for Kievan Rus'.

Harald Hardrada returned to Norway in 1046 and wrestled the throne away from its occupant, Magnus I. Harald would spend years fighting to keep control of Denmark but failed in that effort. Harald started to look at England as a possible conquest.[69]

Harald was a distant relative of Cnut, but he had no direct blood ties to the English crown. He would have to seize England by conquest. An internal dispute improved his chances of doing that.

Tostig Godwinson was the brother of the new king of England, Harold Godwinson. Once the earl of Northumbria, Tostig was overthrown as earl by rebels who received Harold's support (Harold was convinced Tostig could not hold onto Northumbria). Tostig approached Harald with the proposal of having him take the throne of England and restoring Tostig to his earldom. Harald agreed to the idea and began assembling a fleet in the spring of 1066. He sailed from Norway after naming his son, Magnus, his successor.

The Norwegian king landed in England on September 18th, 1066, with approximately fifteen thousand soldiers. He met with Tostig, and the two

---

[69] Dr. Jessica Nelson, P. (2016, January 5). *The death of Edward the Confessor and the conflicting claims to the English Crown*. Retrieved from History.blog.gov.uk: https://history.blog.gov.uk/2016/01/05/the-death-of-edward-the-confessor-and-the-conflicting-claims-to-the-english-crown/.

began their march south. Everything looked to be in their favor because, at the time, Harold Godwinson was anticipating an invasion from Normandy and was on the southern coast.

Harald devastated Scarborough, seized York, and won a victory at Fulford. Harald made the mistake of waiting for York to present him with hostages. He was confident that Harold could not effectively respond. Harald Hardrada was mistaken.[70]

Stamford Bridge

Amazingly, Harold led a forced march from southern England to confront the invasion force in just four days. On September 25th, 1066, Harold surprised Tostig and Harald at Stamford Bridge. The Vikings had left most of their armor behind on their ships. Harold's army charged downhill into the enemy and eventually broke the Viking shield wall.

The result was a massacre. Thousands of Vikings died as confusion took over. Both Harald and Tostig were killed in the fighting. Of the original fleet of three hundred ships, only twenty-four vessels were required to carry the surviving Vikings back to Norway. King Harold's victory was complete.[71]

Stamford Bridge was the last battle fought by the Vikings on English soil. It marked the end of Viking interest in England as a place of plunder or conquest. England was no longer part of Scandinavian politics, and its orientation would increasingly be more focused on mainland Europe. While the battle would be overshadowed by the contest that took place a few weeks later, the Battle of Stamford Bridge marks a turning point in English history.

Hastings

The main man in the 1066 drama was William of Normandy, also known at this time as William the Bastard. There is a claim that Edward the Confessor chose William to be his successor, although there is no hard evidence that this happened. William did have a connection to the

---

[70] Neill, C. (2023, April 17). *Who Was Harald Hardrada? The Norwegian Claimant to the English Throne in 1066*. Retrieved from Historyhit.com: https://www.historyhit.com/1066-harald-hardraada-lands-england/.

[71] Castelow, E. (2023, August 29). *The Battle of Stamford Bridge*. Retrieved from Historic-uk.com: https://www.historic-uk.com/HistoryMagazine/DestinationsUK/The-Battle-of-Stamford-Bridge/.

English throne, though. He was the grandson of Edward's maternal uncle, Richard II of Normandy.

The Bayeux Tapestry tells the story of the Battle of Hastings. William of Normandy believed he was the rightful heir to the English throne because in 1051, or so William claimed, Edward the Confessor promised it to him.

The Bayeux Tapestry tells another story as well. Harold shipwrecked on the Norman coast in 1064 and soon after became a guest of William of Normandy. According to the Bayeux Tapestry's account, Harold swore an oath of allegiance to William and promised to support William's claim to the throne.

The Norman side of events claims that Harold was treacherous and ignored his sworn commitment, giving William the right to fight for what was his. William sailed for England on September 27th and landed at Pevensey.

Harold performed an amazing display of warcraft and leadership. Despite having already marched his men across England in a matter of days and defeating a significant enemy, Harold turned around and marched his army south.

What makes this march outstanding is the conditions under which the Anglo-Saxons moved south. The road conditions were harsher than the worst roads we travel today. It is a testimony to the professionalism of Harold's army that his troops reached London on October 6th, only eleven days after the victory at Stamford Bridge, and moved out a few days later, headed for Hastings.

The battle took place on October 14th, 1066. Despite several cavalry charges, William could not break the Anglo-Saxon shield wall and make any headway. Eventually, the Normans pulled back. The excited Anglo-Saxons gave chase, but the Normans had only been feigning a retreat. The battle turned even bloodier, and Harold was killed by an arrow hitting him in the eye. This caused the Anglo-Saxon forces to disintegrate. William, Duke of Normandy, became known as William the Conqueror. He became the king of England on Christmas Day, 1066.[72]

---

[72] Augustyn, A. (2023, August 23). *Harold II.* Retrieved from Britannica.com: https://www.britannica.com/biography/Harold-II.

Interesting Theories

The engagement permanently changed the trajectory of England's history, but it was not a spur-of-the-moment decision. Events that occurred for decades led to William of Normandy's final choice of invasion as the only viable option. In this section, we will look at what took place regarding the succession and some things historians consider when analyzing what happened.

- The Maneuvers of Edward the Confessor

There are historians who argue that Edward the Confessor was not the simple-minded incompetent of many portrayals. He was a man who experienced the ups and downs of royal politics in the early eleventh century. Edward might have been maneuvering to protect the interests of his kingdom while he was still alive and avoid massive invasions. It is possible Edward was playing one side off against the other.

He could make promises in the dark, knowing that he would not be around to watch the outcome. The Anglo-Saxon succession was different from the rest of Europe, and Edward knew that first-hand. Primogeniture was not always the way the English crown was conferred. Alfred the Great is a classic example. The Anglo-Saxons were willing to bypass the sons of the king and permit the man who was the most capable to sit on the throne. Technically, that meant that even if Edward the Confessor made a promise to Duke William of Normandy, the king knew that the Witan could overrule his choice after his death.

Edward could make promises and assurances to both sides. He was effectively freezing them in doing that. Both Harold and William could sit back and believe he would be the king upon Edward's death. All it took was for the old king to pass away. If Edward made promises, knowing full well that the Witan could overturn the pledge, he might have done so to guarantee that his kingdom was not troubled by one party attempting to seize the throne.[73]

- Harold could have easily won at Hastings under normal conditions

There will always be debate about whether Herald made a promise to William of Normandy regarding the succession. What matters most is that Harold Godwinson was crowned king of England, and William of

---

[73] Dr. Jessica Nelson, P. *The death of Edward the Confessor and the conflicting claims to the English Crown.*

Normandy crossed the water to contest it. Who would have won? Encounter at Hastings. Under normal conditions? We say it would have been Harold, hands down. Here is why.

Anyone who has read the history of the Pacific Theater of World War II can appreciate that amphibious landings are very difficult, especially when contested. The American Marines found out about that at Tarawa and Saipan, among other assaults. William would have had a difficult time succeeding if his fleet had been met on the beach by Harold's waiting army. That the Anglo-Saxons loyal to Harold could march over one hundred miles to Stamford Bridge in three days strongly indicates how tough those men were (they repeated that forced march in going from Stamford Bridge back down to Hastings.).

Harald Hardrada was one of the best military leaders of the eleventh century, and he led a force of seasoned veterans. Harold was able to surprise him and beat him. The morale of Harold's army was likely very high after defeating Hardrada. Williams's invading force was approximately the same size as Hardrada's army, so Harold's men knew they could confront the Normans without worrying too much.

The stronghold of Harold's support was Wessex. And that is where William landed. The people of Wessex would have united around Harold and put up a stubborn resistance. It is essential to remember that England had endured the invasion of Sweyn Forkbeard and other seaborne forces within living memory. They knew from either first-hand experience or the stories handed down to them by grandparents and parents what to expect and how to fight back.

William successfully landed on the beach at Pevensey and fought Harold at Hastings. The Normans were still at a disadvantage during the fighting. The Anglo-Saxon shield wall was a knight killer. William could spend the entire day sending his mounted troops against that wall, and if it did not break, all he would gain were the dead bodies of his own men. Harold could wait the entire day and, at nightfall, command an orderly retreat. William could then be drawn into the countryside to a battlefield of Harold's choosing while being harassed by Wessex partisans all the way. Harold could easily set up an ambush and destroy Williams's army.

- William desperately needed a successful diversion.

William was an illegitimate son and had to fight hard to keep his duchy. Normandy was a scene of constant fighting, and William deserves credit for keeping his enemies at bay.

England was a rich country with very fertile land. William could entice fighting men to join him in a campaign of conquest. Once he had won, William would be able to divide up the land among his winning soldiers. That would entice men to go with him and not stay in Normandy to threaten his holdings. William needed to drain Normandy of its available manpower, and an invasion of England gave him that opportunity.

All this is speculation because the facts overrule what might have been scenarios. What we suggest is that. Edward the Confessor had reason to promise the moon to everybody, Harold had an excellent chance to win at Hastings, and William needed an invasion to secure his existing holdings.

The Days That Followed

Stories sprang up in the 12th century that Harold did not die at Hastings. It was claimed that he recovered from his wounds after two years and then went on a pilgrimage. Harold returned as an older man and lived as a hermit until he revealed his true identity before dying. It is an interesting tale, but it is the stuff of legends.

After William was anointed king of England, he introduced Norman customs to England. French became the language of the nobility, and English foreign policy became more attached to events on the Continent.

The Vikings had been a significant part of English history for over three hundred years. Their political influence died at Stamford Bridge. Even so, the Scandinavian invaders left a legacy that is still present today. But after the Battle of Hastings, it was the Normans who played a significant role in molding England. The Anglo-Saxon language and customs became less important as the years passed, as Norman became the language of the court. Then, that all changed when a royal poet named Geoffrey Chaucer sharpened his writing quill and began to draft a story in Middle English about a group of pilgrims headed to Canterbury. He helped legitimize the use of Middle English in literature.

Chapter Nine: Life of a Viking in England

The Vikings were more than robbers roaming the coasts. Many Vikings were farmers back in Scandinavia. When they were not rowing on the high seas, they were raising crops to feed their families. An increase in the population of Scandinavia caused many to look elsewhere to make a living and seek their fortune. Iceland was one destination, but a bigger one was England.

As the Scandinavians migrated to England, they settled down and made a life in their new home. We want to describe what the life of Vikings who settled in England might have looked like. We will see the day's activities through the eyes of a Viking couple named Olaf and Emma.

The Rooster Crows

It was the start of a new day. It was early spring in what is now Yorkshire, England. The sun had just come up, and the farm animals were stirring, looking for their breakfast. Olaf and Emma got up and moved about on their small farm.

Olaf was in his early thirties. There was a time when he was a crew member on a Viking longship, raiding the English coast. Those days were over. Olaf became a Christian, partly out of religious conviction and partly because he wanted to do business with Christian merchants and tradesmen. He saved enough of the money he had received from selling his loot to buy a small farm, where he made a living for himself and his family.

Emma was in her mid-twenties. She and Olaf had two children. Although life was pretty hard on the farm, she did not mind. She grew up in Norway and was used to working hard for a living.

Olaf and Emma had a small herd of sheep, two cows, and a few chickens. Olaf also had some land that grew barley and rye and pasture land where they could harvest hay and peas.

Anglo-Saxon England was a rural state, so most of the people were employed in farming. Vikings who retired from their sea adventures probably tilled their land, which they might have received for their services to their overlords. The farm would have livestock if a farmer could afford cows or pigs. Winter would have been a slow time, but the rest of the year would be devoted to raising crops. Olaf would have used the winter months to do some woodcarving, and Emma would have weaved woolen cloth.

Conversion to Christianity was not always due to religious convictions. Settled Vikings could see the advantages of becoming a Christian. It would allow them the opportunity to intermingle with other people in England and do some business. Some of the conversions were sincere, while others were not. There were situations where a Viking would convert to Christianity and still worship Odin.

Before the ground was ready for plowing, Olaf and Emma decided to make the trip to York (or Jorvik as the Vikings called the city) and sell some of the wood carvings and cloth they had produced in the dark days of December and January. Olaf approached one of his neighbors, who had a large farm, and asked if he could borrow the man's horse and wagon. The neighbor agreed, provided that Olaf would act as a sokeman and help with his harvest the following autumn. Olaf agreed.

While he conducted this business, Emma asked one of her sisters who lived close by to watch the children and tend the livestock in return for some of the money she would make in Jorvik. When Olaf returned home, he loaded the merchandise into the wagon. After dropping off the children with Emma's sister, the two headed west down a dirt road to York.

The day was pretty warm, and there was a nice breeze. Olaf and Emma took the opportunity to look around and see the sights. The territory had once been a place of violent fighting, but everything was peaceful and had been that way for several years. Their route to York was near the shore of the River Ouse. As the wagon creaked and rumbled along the path, Emma waved at the longships that were sailing down the river toward York. These boats were loaded with trade goods that would be sold in the marketplace.

Harald Hardrada would use the River Ouse to sail up to within eight miles of York. The ability of the Viking longships to sail deep into the countryside had a significant advantage in times of peace. It meant that a city like York could benefit from maritime trade.[74]

Olaf and Emma spent the next few hours chatting and discussing what to do with the farm. Finally, just as the sun was starting to set, they glimpsed the walls of York. The city was only a few miles away.

York had everything a person needed to become wealthy and successful. It was a major market in northern England, as well as a manufacturing center. York was originally a Roman garrison town. By the 11th century, it had become an international trading hub, as evidenced by archaeological excavations of coins from Samarkand and seashells from the Persian Gulf.

How big was this city? Byrhtferth of Ramsey, writing in the year 1000, estimates the population of York was around thirty thousand inhabitants. There is, no doubt, an exaggeration. The Domesday Book suggests a population of closer to ten thousand people. That is still a substantial number, making York the second-largest city in England, trailing only London.[75] Olaf drove the wagon through the open gates of the city just before sundown. The couple was now in the largest community of people they would ever know. Being from the country, Olaf and Emma were impressed by the hustle and bustle of the city. Emma hurriedly crossed herself as they drove past an old stone church. That was not an ordinary place of worship. It was the Church of Saint Peter; it was the home church of the archbishop of York. This church was the epicenter of ecclesiastical authority in northern England.

The Archdiocese of York dates to 735 when Ecgbert, the brother of a king of Northumbria, was granted the pallium and recognized as an archbishop. The Church of Saint Peter survived the Viking invasion of

---

[74] Battlefields Hub. (2023, August 31). *The Viking Invasion.* Retrieved from Battlefieldstrust.com: https://www.battlefieldstrust.com/resource-centre/viking/campainpageview.asp?pageid=541.

[75] Aitcheson, J. (2023, August 31). *York.* Retrieved from Jamesaitcheson.com: https://www.jamesaitcheson.com/england-in-1066/york/.

865, but it was destroyed by the Normans in 1069. The present cathedral, York Minster, was constructed between 1220 and 1472 and is considered a masterpiece of Gothic-style architecture.[76]

It was starting to get dark, and the couple needed to find a place to stay for the night. Emma was nervous because she was afraid that robbers might steal everything they had. Her fear came from the stories she had heard about the people in York. She was told they look nice but not to trust them!

Olaf told her not to worry. He had some friends from his roving days living in York, and they had invited them to stay at their house. Olaf remembered the directions and steered the wagon down the street until he reached their destination. His friends welcomed him and helped take all the merchandise into the house.

Exhausted from the trip, Olaf and Emma fell asleep quickly. The morning would be very busy. They hoped they would have a profitable day.

Off to Market!

Olaf woke up just before sunrise. He moved quietly so that he did not disturb Emma and carefully unpacked the products they wanted to sell that day. Olaf planned to sell what he made in the morning and then return to the market and sell Emma's weaving in the afternoon. He was proud of his wood carvings and had every right to be.

Viking wood carvings are a form of art. They were originally used to decorate houses, boats, and other places. It was the type of work Scandinavians would do during the long winters to while away the hours. The intricate patterns and styles are still used today and taught to enthusiastic hobbyists.[77]

Olaf was equally proud of the work that his wife did. Weaving was very important in English history at that time. Cloth-making was a skill that required patience and dexterity. Various tools, such as the drop spindle, were used to make the yarn and weave the material. Often, those tools were made from wood, bone, or bronze. Natural dyes were used to color the cloth. The process was time-consuming and required

---

[76] History of York. (2023, August 31). *York Minster*. Retrieved from Historyofyork.org: http://www.historyofyork.org.uk/themes/york-minster.
[77] Stryi Carving Tools. (2023, August 31). *Scandinavian Carving*. Retrieved from Stryicarvingtools.com: https://stryicarvingtools.com/blogs/news/scandinavian-carving.

skill. Proficient weavers would produce wall hangings with the soumak technique. Other artisans would use Emma's material to make beautiful clothing and works of art.[78]

The York Market

The first market charter for York was drafted in 700. It specified where the market would be located and on what days it would be held. Only free men were allowed to sell goods.

Temporary stalls would be erected and taken down after the market days. So, in a very prominent place, there would be an open space for a few days, while on other days, it would be packed with tradesmen and merchants selling their wares.

Olaf did not have a stall. However, that did not matter because he was not planning to have a permanent place to sell his products. Instead, he would sell things to merchants, who would then sell them to others. The same was true for Emma's cloth.

Olaf and Emma had been to the York market before, so they knew where to go to sell their merchandise. They visited a few stalls, made some transactions, and by the end of the day, the two had made a fair amount of money for their efforts.[79]

Payment

Olaf and Emma were paid with coins for their merchandise. It is not true that business transactions were all conducted in bartering. Anglo-Saxon England used coins as early as the 7th century when Eadbald of Kent first produced them. The silver penny was a common currency. Although Vikings originally used bullion in transactions, they became more comfortable using coins as they settled deeper into the English social landscape.

Dinner in Those Days

Olaf and Emma returned to their friend's home in time for dinner. It would not be a feast like the nobility would serve, but the food would be filling.

---

[78] Regia Anglorum. (2023, August 31). *Textiles*. Retrieved from Regia.org: https://regia.org/research/life/textiles.htm.

[79] History of York. (2023, August 1). *Trade in the Medieval City*. Retrieved from Historyofyork.org: http://www.historyofyork.org.uk/themes/trade-in-the-medieval-city.

The food was plain in those days because few people could afford to put spices in their meals. Bread was an everyday staple, and it would be cooked in a clay oven. The diet was primarily vegetarian, and onions, turnips, cabbage, and carrots were standard items on the table. Salted fish or eels might be served. Meat, such as mutton, would be served on special occasions.

Fruit was seasonal and was available in the summertime and the fall. Water was polluted and not served at the dinner table. Instead, Olaf and Emma would wash their food down with diluted ale or cider.[80]

Going Home

Olaf and Emma set off for home the following morning. They gave their friends some of the wood carvings and cloth that did not sell. Going home would not take too much time because the wagon was lighter.

Olaf shared with Emma a conversation he had in York with an old friend. Leif was a former crewmate, and he and Olaf had been on several voyages. Leif did not settle down to become a farmer or tradesman. He decided to remain a warrior and was a mercenary. He shared tales of the time he spent in Byzantium as a member of the Varangian Guard.

The Varangian Guard was primarily composed of Norsemen. They were the bodyguards of the Byzantine emperor. Leif spoke of the marvels he saw of the palace and the imperial court in Constantinople. Leif also spent some time in Novgorod, where he protected merchants. Olaf enjoyed the stories but was happy with the life he was leading. His days on the water were in the past.

The Thing

Emma and Olaf were halfway home when they came upon a friend they had not seen for a while. They decided to stop and have a chat with him. The conversation went here and there. Some of the topics were items that had been discussed at the annual thing.

The thing was a Norse tradition. It was a gathering that took place annually and was a central governing body. It was a place where issues could be discussed and legal matters could be decided. Disputes could be peaceably settled. Malefactors could be tried for their alleged crimes.

---

[80] Roller, S. (2023, June 5). *What Did the Anglo-Saxons Eat and Drink?* Retrieved from Historyhit.com: https://www.historyhit.com/anglo-saxon-food-and-drink/.

Fines were often levied on those found guilty.

The fine was known as wergild, which is Old English for "man payment." It was the compensation paid by the guilty party to the injured party or that person's family in the case of death. The social status of the guilty person determined the amount. Thus, a common person's wergild was significantly lower than what was imposed on a rich man.[81]

Olaf winced as he recalled a trial at the thing. Vikings enjoyed hearing legal arguments, and trials were common whenever thing was convened. They would have twelve hereditary lawmen who would listen to cases, and freedmen were formed into committees during the court sessions. These were the origins of the jury system in Anglo-Saxon England. Æthelred the Unready helped to advance the concept of trial by jury with a legal code stipulating that twelve leading thegns (minor nobles) of each wapentake would investigate crimes without bias. Henry II would later formalize this process into the jury system.

Emma chuckled at Olaf's comments. She, too, had witnessed that trial, and it had a special meaning for her. It involved a woman who had a complaint about how a man was trying to take over her property. Viking women had rights that were unheard of in other parts of Europe. They could own property, and they could inherit their parent's estate. Viking women were permitted to make their own choices, which included their marriage partners and possessions. They could hold positions of power and authority in the community.

The couple said goodbye to their neighbor and drove on. They passed several people on the trail, and Emma noticed something that was making her feel uncomfortable. Vikings and Anglo-Saxons usually got along together, but Emma saw many frowns on the faces of the people passing by. She mentioned her concerns to her husband, and Olaf nodded his head solemnly.

The Danelaw was no more and had been gone for years. Still, people remembered the days when raids into Wessex brought about the Danelaw, and those memories died hard. Some priests were skeptical of Viking conversions and suspected that people were still practicing pagan rights in the dark.

---

[81] Nolen, J. L. (2023, August 31). *Wergild*. Retrieved from Britannica.com: https://www.britannica.com/topic/wergild.

Olaf remembered the conversations he had with a friend at the thing. King Æthelred the Unready was worried about the loyalty of the Danes in his kingdom. The ruler was starting to wonder if they were traitors. The Anglo-Saxons all appeared to worry that former Vikings wanted to return to the days when they had significant power. Olaf was deeply concerned that troubled times were coming. He did not repeat that conversation to his wife and tried to calm her down. Still, he was worried.

They finally reached their relative's house and gathered up their children. Emma's sister drove the wagon, and the family sat in the back as passengers. Once they got back to their farm, Emma and the children went inside the house. Olaf walked over to a small shed where he kept his tools.

Once inside the shack, Olaf looked around, trying to find something. Finally, he saw a piece of Emma's cloth wrapped around something. He picked up the bundle and took off the weavings to expose its contents. It was his old battle ax. When he stopped his sea-roving days, Olaf did not leave his tools behind. The battle ax looked a little dull, but it could be sharpened until the weapon was once again deadly.

Olaf looked around the shed. In a corner, behind some farm tools, was his old shield. That was still usable. He chewed on his lower lip as dark thoughts came through his mind.

Leif had tried to persuade him to become a mercenary in Rus', but Olaf had declined. He was happy with his new life, but he was not pleased with the way things were going. His Anglo-Saxon neighbors were starting to act hostile to him. It would not take much for King Æthelred to turn on his Danish subjects. Some people would be willing to do the king's dirty work. Olaf did not like to think of it, but if anyone tried to harm his family, that fool would find out there was still some of the old berserker lurking inside him, waiting to break free.

Olaf would allow no one to destroy what he and Emma had worked so hard to create. He looked down at the floor of the shed, looking for something else. It was a whetstone. Silently, he applied the whetstone to the blade of his battle ax, sharpening the weapon until it was battle-ready.

Conclusion

The Viking era lasted a little over three hundred years, but significant changes to England occurred. The country went from four kingdoms to one unified state. That is a considerable accomplishment when one compares England with the rest of medieval Europe. Countries such as France or Spain would not be united until centuries later.

There are many components to the Vikings' story. When reading about the Vikings, it is essential to remember that some of the early accounts were written by men who had no reason to cast the Norsemen in a favorable light. Modern research and archaeology have given us a better picture of those who lived in medieval Scandinavia. The times were rough, but people were not savages. They were something far different.

England, as a nation, made substantial strides. It was a nation of laws when William the Conqueror set foot on the shore near Hastings. Charters and law codes replaced traditions and rituals as instruments of administration and justice. The Vikings have a right to claim some of these developments with the innovations they introduced.

We are not saying that the Vikings and the Anglo-Saxons turned England into an urban sprawl. However, both of them contributed to creating urban centers that did not exist before. Granted, it would be centuries before England lost its rural composition. However, the burghs and boroughs brought the benefits of urban settings and relatively large populations to England.

Norse mythology has enriched English literature for thousands of years. We still read works that Viking stories have influenced in the books of. J. R. R. Tolkien and Neil Gaiman. Cable network programs like *Game of Thrones* and *Vikings* are full of references to legends that originated in Scandinavia.

Geoffrey Chaucer wrote in a language that had become a potpourri of phrases and words gleaned from various groups that came to England. A rich language was created with a linguistic base in Old English, French, and Norse. Many of us speak without noticing the origins of nouns, pronouns, adjectives, verbs, and adverbs. The Vikings contributed significantly to our modern vocabulary.

Viking artwork evolved over the centuries, and the influence of Viking designs has appeared in English artwork. Viking art can still be seen in various designs today, from jewelry to graphic design, especially computer games.

This is just a taste of how the Vikings influenced England. Needless to say, the Viking era was a formative period. Modern society has foundations produced by two cultures coming together. In a way, the diversity of the English society strengthened the nation, as it birthed a culture reflecting a willingness to learn rather than resist outside influences. A tradition of assimilation, not segregation, is an enduring legacy from this time.

If you enjoyed this book, a review on Amazon would be greatly appreciated because it would mean a lot to hear from you.

To leave a review:
1. Open your camera app.
2. Point your mobile device at the QR code.
3. The review page will appear in your web browser.

Thanks for your support!

Here's another book by Enthralling History that you might like

Free limited time bonus

Stop for a moment. We have a free bonus set up for you. The problem is this: we forget 90% of everything that we read after 7 days. Crazy fact, right? Here's the solution: we've created a printable, 1-page pdf summary for this book that you're reading now. All you have to do to get your free pdf summary is to go to the following website:

https://livetolearn.lpages.co/enthrallinghistory/

Once you do, it will be intuitive. Enjoy, and thank you!

Bibliography

Abernethy, S. (2014, January 24). *Cnut England's Danish King.* Retrieved from The Freelance History Writer: https://thefreelancehistorywriter.com/2014/01/24/cnut-englands-danish-king/.

Aitcheson, J. (2023, August 31). *York.* Retrieved from Jamesaitcheson.com: https://www.jamesaitcheson.com/england-in-1066/york/.

Anglo-Saxon.net. (2023, August 21). *Early-Medieval-England.net Timeline: 871-899.* Retrieved from Anglo-Saxon.net: http://www.anglo-saxons.net/hwaet/?do=seek&query=871-899.

Anglo-Saxons.net. (2023, August 26). *Edward the Elder.* Retrieved from Early-Medieval-England: http://www.anglo-saxons.net/hwaet/?do=get&type=person&id=EdwardtheElder.

Augustyn, A. (2023, August 23). *Harold II.* Retrieved from Britannica.com: https://www.britannica.com/biography/Harold-II.

Battlefields Hub. (2023, August 31). *The Viking Invasion.* Retrieved from Battlefieldstrust.com: https://www.battlefieldstrust.com/resource-centre/viking/campainpageview.asp?pageid=541.

Baxter, Stephen (2009). "Edward the Confessor and the Succession Question". In Mortimer, Richard (ed.). Edward the Confessor: The Man and the Legend. Woodbridge: Boydell Press.

Bishop, C. (2021, March 18). *Horses in battle at the time of Alfred the Great.* Retrieved from Historiamag.com: https://www.historiamag.com/horses-in-battle-at-the-time-of-alfred-the-great/#:~:text=King%20Edmund%20of%20East%20Anglia,of%20the%20horses%20they%20needed.

Brain, J. (2023, August 29). *Edward the Confessor.* Retrieved from Historic-uk.com: https://www.historic-uk.com/HistoryUK/HistoryofEngland/Edward-The-Confessor/.

Brain, J. (2023, August 27). *King Æthelred The Unready.* Retrieved from Historic-uk.com: https://www.historic-uk.com/HistoryUK/HistoryofEngland/Æthelred-The-Unready/.

Brain, J. (2023, August 26). *The Five Boroughs of Danelaw.* Retrieved from Historic-uk.com: https://www.historic-uk.com/HistoryUK/HistoryofEngland/The-Five-Boroughs-Of-Danelaw/.

Britain Express. (2023, August 20). *Viking York.* Retrieved from Britainexpress.com: https://www.britainexpress.com/cities/york/viking.htm.

Butler, J. (2023, August 29). *The Real Ragnar Lothbrok.* Retrieved from Histori-uk.com: https://www.historic-uk.com/HistoryUK/HistoryofEngland/Ragnar-Lothbrok/#:~:text=This%20may%20well%20have%20been,settlement%20not%20far%20from%20Dublin.

Castelow, E. (2023, August 29). *The Battle of Stamford Bridge.* Retrieved from Historic-uk.com: https://www.historic-uk.com/HistoryMagazine/DestinationsUK/The-Battle-of-Stamford-Bridge/.

Cavendish, R. (2002, November). *The St. Brice's Day Massacre.* Retrieved from History Today: https://www.historytoday.com/archive/st-brice%E2%80%99s-day-massacre.

Cerdic. (2023, August 21). *Treaty Of Wedmore 878-890.* Retrieved from The History of England: https://thehistoryofengland.co.uk/resource/treaty-of-wedmore-878-890/

Chakra, H. (2021, September 27). *The Story of Danelaw.* Retrieved from About-history.com: https://about-history.com/the-story-of-danelaw/.

Curry, A. (2017). *How to Fight Like a Viking.* Retrieved from Nationalgeographic.com: https://www.nationalgeographic.com/history/article/vikings-fight-warfare-battle-weapons.

Davidson, Michael R. (2001). "The (Non)submission of the Northern Kings in 920." In Higham, N. J.; Hill, D. H. (eds.). Edward the Elder, 899–924. Abingdon, UK: Routledge. pp. 200–211.

Discover Middle Ages. (2023, August 31). *Viking Ships.* Retrieved from Discovermiddleages.co.uk: https://www.discovermiddleages.co.uk/medieval-life/viking-ships/.

Discovery. (2023, May 3). *Who was King Burgred of Mercia and what did he do?* Retrieved from Discoveryuk.com: https://www.discoveryuk.com/monarchs-and-rulers/who-was-king-burgred-of-mercia-and-what-did-he-do/.

Dorothy Whitlock, W. A. (2023, August 10). *The Period of the Scandinavian Invasions.* Retrieved from Britannica.com: https://www.britannica.com/place/United-Kingdom/The-church-and-the-monastic-revival.

Dr. Jessica Nelson, P. (2016, January 5). *The death of Edward the Confessor and the conflicting claims to the English Crown.* Retrieved from History.blog.gov.uk: https://history.blog.gov.uk/2016/01/05/the-death-of-edward-the-confessor-and-the-conflicting-claims-to-the-english-crown/.

Douglas, David C. (1990). *William the Conqueror: The Norman Impact Upon England.* London: Methuen.

"Edward the Elder." http://www.anglo-saxons.net/hwaet/?do=get&type=person&id=EdwardtheElder.

E. H. Seigfried, K. (2015, November 6). *The Battle of Maldon.* Retrieved from The Norse Mythology Blog: https://www.norsemyth.org/2015/11/the-battle-of-maldon.html.

England's North East. (203, August 10). *Northumbria's Downfall.* Retrieved from Englandsnortheast.co.uk: https://englandsnortheast.co.uk/northumbria-anarchy/.

English Heritage. (2023, August 10). *Early Christianity in Anglo-Saxon Northumbria.* Retrieved from English-heritage.org.uk: https://www.english-heritage.org.uk/visit/places/lindisfarne-priory/History/.

English History. (2023, August 27). *Sweyn Forkbeard.* Retrieved from Englishhistory.net: https://englishhistory.net/vikings/sweyn-forkbeard/.

English Monarchs. (2023, August 20). *The Danelaw.* Retrieved from Englishmonarchs.com: https://www.englishmonarchs.co.uk/vikings_11.html

English Monarchs. (2023, August 23). *The Battle of Brunanburh.* Retrieved from Englishmonarchs.co.uk: https://www.englishmonarchs.co.uk/brunanburh.html.

Erenow.net. (2023, August 26). *The Danelaw II.* Retrieved from Erenow.net: https://erenow.net/postclassical/thevikingsahistory/12.php.

European Royal History. (2022, October 22). *October 26, 899: Death of Alfred the Great, King of the Anglo-Saxons.* Retrieved from Europeanroyalhistory.com: https://europeanroyalhistory.wordpress.com//?s=Alfred+the+Great&search=Go.

Fi, B. a. (2015, May 2). *Vikings in the Danelaw.* Retrieved from Babiafi.co.uk: https://www.babiafi.co.uk/2015/05/vikings-in-danelaw.html.

Garner, T. (2018, January 2). *Michael Wood on Æthelstan's "Great War" to Unite Anglo-Saxon England.* Retrieved from Historyanswers.co.uk:

https://www.historyanswers.co.uk/history-of-war/michael-wood-on-Æthelstans-great-war-to-unite-anglo-saxon-england/.

Giles, J.A. (1914). *The Anglo-Saxon Chronicle.* London: G. Bell and Sonson.

Henriques, M. (2023, July 25). *The Enduring Influence of Norse Mythology on Contemporary Culture.* Retrieved from Medium.com: https://medium.com/new-earth-consciousness/the-enduring-influence-of-norse-mythology-on-contemporary-culture-2e32cd2e3489

History of York. (2023, August 1). *Trade in the Medieval City.* Retrieved from Historyofyork.org: http://www.historyofyork.org.uk/themes/trade-in-the-medieval-city.

History of York. (2023, August 31). *York Minster.* Retrieved from Historyofyork.org: http://www.historyofyork.org.uk/themes/york-minster.

History-maps.com. (2023, August 10). *Viking Invasions of England.* Retrieved from History-maps.com: https://history-maps.com/story/Viking-Invasions-of-England.

Irvine, A. (2022, December). *10 Facts About Viking Warrior Ragnar Lodbrok.* Retrieved from Historyhit.com: https://www.historyhit.com/facts-about-viking-ragnar-lodbrok/.

Kruljac, I. (2022, August 20). *The Great Heathen Army: What was it, and how did it unite the Vikings?* Retrieved from Thevikingherald.com: https://thevikingherald.com/article/the-great-heathen-army-what-was-it-and-how-did-it-unite-the-vikings/76.

Legends and Chronicles. (2023, August 20). *Viking Children.* Retrieved from legendsandchronicles.com: https://www.legendsandchronicles.com/ancient-civilizations/the-vikings/viking-children/.

Lewis, R. (2023, August 20). *Ivar the Boneless.* Retrieved from Brittanica.com: https://www.britannica.com/biography/Ivar-the-Boneless.

MacNeil, R. (2019, May). *The Great Heathen Failure: Why the Great Heathen Army Failed to Conquer the Whole of Anglo-Saxon England.* Retrieved from Digitalcommons.winthrop.edu: https://digitalcommons.winthrop.edu/cgi/viewcontent.cgi?article=1105&context=graduatetheses.

Maddicott, John (2010). The Origins of the English Parliament, 924–1327. Oxford, UK: Oxford University Press.

Marsh, A. (2022, June 21). *In 793 AD, Vikings attacked Lindisfarne. Here's why it was so shocking.* Retrieved from National Geographic.co.uk: https://www.nationalgeographic.co.uk/history-and-civilisation/2022/06/in-793ad-vikings-attacked-lindisfarne-heres-why-it-was-so-shocking.

Medieval Archives. (2020, November 20). *King Edmund the Martyr Killed by the Great Heathen Army.* Retrieved from Medievalarchives.com: https://medievalarchives.com/2020/11/20/king-edmund-the-martyr-killed-by-the-great-heathen-army/.

Meyer, I. (2021, July 31). *Viking Art-The History of Norse and Viking Artwork.* Retrieved from Artincontext.org: https://artincontext.org/viking-art/

Mingren, W. (2020, May 21). *Cnut the Great: The Myth, the Man, and the Multi-National Viking Monarch.* Retrieved from Ancient Origins: https://www.ancient-origins.net/history-famous-people/cnut-great-0013741.

Neill, C. (2023, April 17). *Who Was Harald Hardrada? The Norwegian Claimant to the English Throne in 1066.* Retrieved from Historyhit.com: https://www.historyhit.com/1066-harald-hardraada-lands-england/.

New Advent. (2023, August 20). *St. Edmund the Martyr.* Retrieved from Newadvent.org: https://www.newadvent.org/cathen/05295a.htm.

Nolen, J. L. (2023, August 31). *Wergild.* Retrieved from Britannica.com: https://www.britannica.com/topic/wergild.

"Order of Medieval Women."
https://www.medievalwomen.org/aeligthelflaeligdnbspladv-of-the-mercians.html.

Ortenberg, Veronica (2010). "The King from Overseas: Why did Æthelstan Matter in Tenth-Century Continental Affairs?" In Rollason, David; Leyser, Conrad; Williams, Hannah (eds.). England and the Continent in the Tenth Century: Studies in Honour of Wilhelm.

Parker, E. (2016, October). *Cnut: The Great Dane.* Retrieved from History Extra: https://www.historyextra.com/period/anglo-saxon/king-cnut-danish-why-called-great-rule-england-success/.

Pearce, S. (2023, February 16). *Where King Alfred Burnt Cakes in Athelney-King Alfred's Monument!* Retrieved from Third Eye Traveler: https://thirdeyetraveller.com/where-king-alfred-burnt-cakes-in-athelney-king-alfreds-monument/.

Regia Anglorum. (2023, August 31). *Textiles.* Retrieved from Regia.org: https://regia.org/research/life/textiles.htm.

Roller, S. (2023, June 5). *What Did the Anglo-Saxons Eat and Drink?* Retrieved from Historyhit.com: https://www.historyhit.com/anglo-saxon-food-and-drink/.

Ross, D. (2023, August 26). *King Æthelstan.* Retrieved from Britainexpress.com: https://www.britainexpress.com/History/Æthelstan.htm.

Ross, D. (2023, August 21). *The Battle of Edington.* Retrieved from Britain Express: https://www.britainexpress.com/History/battles/edington.htm.

Roua, V. (2016, May 7). *A Brief History of the Danish Vikings and of the Danelaw.* Retrieved from Thedockyards.com:

https://www.thedockyards.com/the-danish-vikings-and-the-danelaw/.

Shipfans.blogspot.com. (2023, August 10). *Drakkar Viking Ship 9th-132th century.* Retrieved from Shipfans.blogspot.com: http://shipfans.blogspot.com/2010/04/drakkar-viking-ship-9th-13th-century.html

Skald, F. t. (2016, September 16). *Viking History: Post-by-Post.* Retrieved from Fjorn-the-skald.tumblr.com: https://fjorn-the-skald.tumblr.com/post/150515624715/lesson-16-viking-money-commerce-coins-and.

Skjaden. (2020, January 16). *Trade in the Viking Age-Do You Know Which Trade Towns That Were the Most Important Ones?* Retrieved from Nordic Culture: https://skjalden.com/where-did-the-vikings-trade/.

Sky History. (2023, August 20). *11 Facts About Fearsome Viking "Ivar the Boneless."* Retrieved from www.history.co.uk: https://www.history.co.uk/articles/11-facts-about-fearsome-viking-ivar-the-boneless.

Sky History. (2023, August 26). *Old Norse Words We Use Every Day.* Retrieved from www.history.co.uk: https://www.history.co.uk/shows/vikings/articles/old-norse-words-we-use-every-day.

Sky History. (2023, August 20). *Who Was Viking Legend Bjorn Ironside.* Retrieved from History.co.uk: https://www.history.co.uk/articles/who-was-viking-legend-bjorn-ironside

Stryi Carving Tools. (2023, August 31). *Scandinavian Carving.* Retrieved from Stryicarvingtools.com: https://stryicarvingtools.com/blogs/news/scandinavian-carving.

The History Junkie. (2023, August 21). *5 Reasons That Burhs Were Important and How They Helped Alfred the Great Defeat the Vikings.* Retrieved from Thehistoryjunkie.com: https://thehistoryjunkie.com/5-reasons-that-burhs-were-important-and-how-they-helped-alfred-the-great-defeat-the-vikings/.

The Ministry of History. (2020, May 5). *Ragnar Lothbrok.* Retrieved from Theministryofhistory.co.uk: https://www.theministryofhistory.co.uk/historical-biographies/ragnarlothbrok.

The Viking Answer Lady. (2023, August 29). *Origin of the phrase, "A furore Normannorum libera nos, Domine.* Retrieved from The Viking Answer Lady: http://www.vikinganswerlady.com/vikfury.shtml.

Thomsen, M. H. (2023, August 10). *Instrument navigation in the Viking Age?* Retrieved from Vikingeskibs Muskeet: https://www.vikingeskibsmuseet.dk/en/professions/education/knowledge-of-sailing/instrument-navigation-in-the-viking-age.

Trow, M. J. (2005), *Cnut - Emperor of the North,* Stroud: Sutton.

Ulvog, J. (2017, November 8). *Size of Viking raiding parties.* Retrieved from Ancientfinances.com: https://ancientfinances.com/2017/11/08/size-of-viking-raiding-parties/#:~:text=In%20The%20Vikings%20course%20from,500%20up%20to%201%2C200%20warriors.

Viking.no. (2004, August 14). *The Danelaw: Population, culture and heritage.* Retrieved from Viking.no: https://www.viking.no/e/england/danelaw/e-heritage-danelaw.htm.

Viking.no. (2004, August 14). *Trade routes in the British Isles.* Retrieved from Viking.no: https://www.viking.no/e/england/york/jorvik_trading_centre_2.html.

Warriors & Legends. (2023, August 20). *Viking Warrior Raids.* Retrieved from Warriorsandlegends.com: https://www.warriorsandlegends.com/viking-warriors/viking-warrior-raids/.

Warriors and Legends.com. (2023, August 31). *Famous Viking Warriors.* Retrieved from Warriorsandlegends.com: https://www.warriorsandlegends.com/viking-warriors/famous-viking-warriors/.

Williamson, J. (2022, August 20). *Who was Ubba Ragnarsson, the Viking commander of the Great Heathen Army?* Retrieved from Thevikingherald.com: https://thevikingherald.com/article/who-was-ubba-ragnarsson-the-viking-commander-of-the-great-heathen-army/194.

Zimmerman, M. (2023, August 29). *Earl Godwin, The Lesser Known Kingmaker.* Retrieved from Historic-uk.com: https://www.historic-uk.com/HistoryUK/HistoryofEngland/Earl-Godwin/.

www.ingramcontent.com/pod-product-compliance
Lightning Source LLC
LaVergne TN
LVHW051746080426
835511LV00018B/3246